Developing Countries and the Multilateral Trading System

Developing Countries and the Multilateral Trading System

From the GATT to the Uruguay Round and the Future

T. N. Srinivasan

WestviewPress

A Division of HarperCollins*Publishers*

Copyright © 1998 by Westview Press, A Division of HarperCollins Publishers, Inc.

LKP

Published in 1998 in the United States of America by Westview Press, 5500 Central Avenue, Boulder, Colorado 80301-2877, and in the United Kingdom by Westview Press, 12 Hid's Copse Road, Cumnor Hill, Oxford OX2 9JJ

A CIP catalog record for this book is available from the Library of Congress.
ISBN 0-8133-3419-5

The paper used in this publication meets the requirements of the American National Standard for Permanence of Paper for Printed Library Materials Z39.48-1984.

10   9   8   7   6   5   4   3   2   1

Contents

Preface

In summer 1995, I was invited by the Economic Development Institute (EDI) of the World Bank to write a paper on the external environment for the developing countries following the conclusion of the Uruguay Round of Multilateral Trade Negotiations in April 1994. As I began my research, I found myself increasingly drawn to the tussle between the opposing ideas of insulation from and integration with the world economy in the developing countries, both in their attitudes toward and actions in the General Agreement on Tariffs and Trade (GATT) as well as in their role in successive rounds of multilateral trade negotiations (MTNs) sponsored by the GATT. This book is the result. It places the agreement at the Uruguay Round in historical perspective. Its focus is on the interaction between the developed and developing countries on matters relating to the global trading system and its disciplines since the founding of GATT.

I thank Isabel Guerrero, Jayanta Roy, and Vinod Thomas for inviting me and providing a friendly, hospitable, and stimulating environment at the EDI for my research. I thank Michael Finger, Isabel Guerrero, Bernhard Gunter, Bernard Hoekman, Robert Hudec, Anne Krueger, Philip Levy, Will Martin, Jayanta Roy, Vinod Thomas, and Alan Winters for their valuable comments on an earlier draft. I am grateful to Sanjay Desilva, Vandana Sipahimalani, and Beata Smarzynska for carefully editing the manuscript and for research assistance. My debts to my secretary, Louise Danishevsky, are too numerous to enumerate here.

I am grateful to the World Bank, the Ford Foundation (under Grant 950-1341 to the Economic Growth Center, Yale University), and the Center for Research on Economic Development and Policy Reform at Stanford University (where Chapter 12 was written) for financial support.

None of the commentators and research assistants are responsible for the views expressed in this book. The findings, interpretation, and conclusions are entirely mine and should not be attributed in any manner to the World Bank, to its affiliated organizations, or to members of its board of executive directors or to the countries they represent. The same disclaimer applies with respect to the Ford Foundation, the Center for Research on Economic Development and Policy Reform of Stanford University, and the Economic Growth Center of Yale University.

T. N. Srinivasan

Acronyms

AD	antidumping
ADD	antidumping duty
ADE	Asian developing economies
ADM	antidumping measures
APEC	Asia-Pacific Economic Cooperation
APFTA	Asia-Pacific Free Trade Area
ASEAN	Association of Southeast Asian Nations
ATC	Agreement on Textiles and Clothing
BEM	big emerging markets
BOP	balance of payments
CCII	cross-country intraindustry
CEPAL	UN Commission for Latin America
CMEA	Council of Mutual Economic Assistance
CTG	Council on Trade in Goods
CU	customs union
DS	dispute settlement
DSB	Dispute Settlement Body
DSM	dispute-settlement mechanism
DSU	Dispute Settlement Understanding
EC	European Community
ECOSOC	Economic and Social Council
EFTA	European Free Trade Area
EU	European Union
FDI	foreign direct investment
FTA	free trade area
G-7	Group of Seven
GATS	General Agreement on Trade in Services
GATT	General Agreement on Tariffs and Trade
GF	Group of Forty
GN	Group of Nine
GNS	Group of Negotiations on Services
GSP	Generalized System of Preferences
GT	Group of Ten
HIC	high-income countries

ILO	International Labor Organization
IMF	International Monetary Fund
IT	information technology
ITO	International Trade Organization
MERCOSUR	Preferential Trade Arrangement Between Argentina, Brazil, Paraguay, and Uruguay
MFA	Multifibre Arrangement
MFN	most favored nation
MITI	Ministry of International Trade and Industry
MTN	Multilateral Trade Negotiation
NAFTA	North American Free Trade Area
NT	National Treatment
NTM	nontariff measure
OECD	Organization for Economic Cooperation and Development
PTA	preferential trading arrangement
QR	quantitative restriction
ROOs	rules of origin
RTA	regional trading agreement
SAL	structural adjustment loan
SAPTA	South Asian Preferential Trade Area
SECAL	sectoral adjustment loan
SGA	safeguards agreement
SGM	safeguard measure
TAFTA	Transatlantic Free Trade Area
TMB	Textiles Monitoring Body
TNC	Trade Negotiating Committee
TRIMs	Trade-Related Investment Measures
TRIPs	Trade-Related Intellectual Property Rights
UN	United Nations
UNCTAD	United Nations Conference on Trade and Development
UNDP	United Nations Development Program
UR	Uruguay Round
VER	voluntary export restraints
VIE	voluntary import expansion
WHO	World Health Organization
WIPO	World Intellectual Property Organization
WTO	World Trade Organization

1　*Introduction*

The Uruguay Round (UR) of the multilateral trade negotiations (MTNs), the latest, eighth, and most ambitious of a series of such negotiations, was formally concluded with the signing on April 15, 1994, at Marrakech, Morocco, of the Final Act, which embodies all the multilateral and plurilateral agreements of the round. The first round, held in Geneva in 1947, resulted in the General Agreement on Tariffs and Trade (GATT). The UR agreements extended multilateral rules and disciplines to trade in services, trade-related aspects of intellectual property rights, and investment measures. They also brought trade in agriculture and textiles back into the GATT. The Final Act included the decision to establish a formal organization called the World Trade Organization (WTO) "to provide the common institutional framework for the conduct of trade relations among its members in matters related to the (Uruguay Round) agreements" (GATT 1994: 6). Ministers representing the 124 governments and the European communities that participated in the UR affirmed in their declaration at the signing of the Final Act "that the establishment of the World Trade Organization (WTO) ushers in a new era of global economic cooperation, reflecting the widespread desire to operate in a fairer and more open multilateral trading system for the benefit and welfare of their peoples" (GATT 1994: iv).

Concentrated protectionist producer interests often have considerably more political power within countries as compared to diffused consumer interests. Negotiations under the GATT have served to redress this imbalance in political power *within countries* through reciprocal liberalization of trade barriers *between countries*. All the eight rounds of the MTNs, including the UR, reduced tariff barriers. The last two, the Tokyo Round and the UR, attempted to set up discipline guidelines regarding the use of nontariff barriers. An important aspect of the evaluation of the UR is the quantitative impact of the reduction of trade barriers on the volume of trade and on welfare in the short and long run. A number of studies attempt to do precisely that, and in Chapter 5, I will briefly turn to them.

1

But an equally, if not more important, though not quantifiable, impact of the UR is its potential effect on the rules of the game, so to speak, in restraining both powerful actors who may be tempted to take advantage of the weak and weak countries that may want to "free ride" on the commitment of the powerful to the system. The developed countries are admittedly powerful and developing countries weak in this sense.

The purpose of this book is not simply to assess the success and failures of the UR per se but also to pursue a much broader theme, namely the interaction between developing countries and the multilateral trading system since the end of World War II and to place the UR in that context. I view this broader theme to be extremely pertinent, since the developing countries have had an ambivalent attitude to the GATT, and their attitude toward integrating their economies with the global trading system has evolved from one of hostility to active promotion. Pursuit of this theme requires a review of history from the beginnings of the GATT to the establishment of the WTO and, in particular, of the negotiations in which developing countries played an active part.

The GATT originated in the failure of some countries, most important, of the United States, to ratify the charter for the International Trade Organization (ITO), which was adopted by the United Nations Conference on Trade and Employment held in Havana, Cuba, during November 1947–March 1948 (hereafter, the Havana conference). The ITO, the International Monetary Fund (IMF), and the World Bank were meant to be the three premier international institutions governing economic relations among countries in the post–World War II era. Technically, since its inception in 1947 and until being subsumed under the WTO in 1994, the GATT was a multilateral agreement (general agreement) among its contracting parties rather than a treaty among sovereign nations. These numbered 23 in 1947 and nearly 100 at the start of the UR in 1986. The GATT enabled the contracting parties to reduce tariffs reciprocally and obliged them through a set of "general clauses" to refrain from taking trade-impeding measures that would reduce the value of the agreed-upon tariff reduction. It included a dispute-settlement mechanism (that in later practice turned out to be weak). Even the application of the GATT as an agreement continued to be provisional from its inception to its very end. The lack of a formal international institution or organization with universal membership and well-defined rules for decisionmaking and enforcement procedures for international commerce has been viewed by many as hampering the progress toward a nondiscriminatory and liberal world trading order. In assessing whether the WTO will serve this role, I must go back to the history of the GATT and the unratified charter of the ITO, if only to see whether the flaws of the GATT have been rectified in the WTO. I do this in Chapter 2.

Developing countries, though never a monolithic bloc, have shared a certain ambivalence toward the GATT from its inception. The original twenty-three contracting parties of the 1947 GATT included the following eleven developing countries: Brazil, Burma (now Myanmar), Ceylon (now Sri Lanka), Chile, China, Cuba, India, Lebanon, Pakistan, Southern Rhodesia (now Zimbabwe), and Syria. Burma, Ceylon, and Southern Rhodesia were not independent then. This group of twenty-three was also the preparatory committee for the Havana conference as well as the committee that drafted the charter for the ITO for discussion at the conference. Fifty-six countries, including thirty developing countries, participated in the conference. Initially, the developing countries condemned the draft submitted by the preparatory committee as serving the interests of the developed countries and holding no hopes for development. Nonetheless, except for Argentina and Poland, all the other countries approved the charter that emerged at the end of the conference. As noted earlier, the charter was not ratified by the United States, and the ITO did not come into being; instead, the treaty on tariff reductions, namely the GATT, came to be provisionally applied.

In their decisionmaking, the contracting parties of the GATT have almost always adopted a consensus procedure in spite of the fact that Article XXV of the GATT required only a simple majority of votes cast for a decision with each contracting party having one vote. Thus in principle, developing countries could have had a significant influence in the GATT decisions. Nonetheless, they tended to view the GATT as promoting the interests of developed countries. Indeed, the first United Nations Conference on Trade and Development (UNCTAD) in 1964, subsequently institutionalized as a "permanent organ" of the General Assembly of the United Nations, provided a forum in which developing countries tried to evolve and articulate a common position on matters relating to trade. The GATT was not intended to be such a forum and had an oversight role in trade matters that UNCTAD never had. Until the Tokyo Round of trade negotiations, many developing countries did not participate effectively, and they had no significant influence on the outcomes of the earlier rounds. They had some influence on the outcomes of the Tokyo Round, where they were united, though not necessarily in ways that served their long-term interests. They chose to participate much more actively and had a greater influence on the final UR agreement. It is therefore worthwhile to analyze the evolution not only of the participation of developing countries in the GATT but also of the incorporation of concerns for development in the articles of the GATT. Such an analysis, to which Chapter 3 is devoted, should help in assessing the potential of the WTO as a guarantor not only of a rule-based global trading order that protects the economically less powerful developing countries but also of their active participation in the making and enforcing of decisions that affect international commerce.

The UR—from its formal authorization by the GATT ministerial conference in September 1986 at Punta del Este, Uruguay, to its formal conclusion in April 1994 at Marrakech, Morocco, with the signing of the Final Act by ministers—was the longest of the eight rounds of the MTNs. A look at its tortuous negotiating history with near breakdowns, changes of negotiating positions by parties, and so on is not only fascinating for its own sake but also helpful in highlighting the basic conflicts of interest among the parties and their political-economy foundations. Clearly, any multilateral agreement is by definition a compromise that the parties found acceptable. As with all compromises, there is the issue of whether the UR agreement is simply a fragile papering over of conflicts that have not been resolved and that are likely to erupt in the future to unravel it or whether it is robust with a significant narrowing, if not a complete resolution, of differences among parties through give-and-take acceptable to each. A brief negotiating history of the UR is provided in Chapter 4.

The UR negotiating agenda was the most ambitious of all rounds. Besides including traditional GATT concerns of reducing barriers at the border on goods trade and extending the GATT disciplines to trade in those goods, for example, agricultural goods, textiles, and apparel, which had not until then been subject to the same disciplines that applied to trade in manufactures, the agenda included strengthening dispute-settlement mechanisms and disciplinary measures regarding safeguards (i.e., antidumping and countervailing-duties measures) as well as the so-called new issues, such as trade in services, trade-related intellectual property, and investment measures. As mentioned earlier, a quantitative assessment of the benefits of trade-barrier reductions is provided in Chapter 5. Chapter 6 takes a brief critical look at the agreements reached on other issues.[1]

The popularity of regional economic integration through preferential trading and investment agreements among countries that often, though not always, are close to each other geographically revived in the late 1980s (with the signing of the North American Free Trade Agreement [NAFTA] among Canada, the United States, and Mexico and MERCOSUR [Preferential Trade Agreement Between Argentina, Brazil, Paraguay, and Uruguay]) in spite of the fact that such attempts by developing countries in the 1960s and 1970s had failed. This revival of interest was understandable when the prospects of concluding the UR with an agreement seemed dim and it looked as if the global trading system would collapse into a set of warring trade blocs. It then made sense for a developing country to seek to become part of a trade bloc with some industrialized country to avoid being marginalized. Seemingly paradoxically, the interest in concluding regional agreements gathered further steam after the successful completion of the UR: NAFTA is likely to open membership negotiations with Chile; a transatlantic free trade agreement (TAFTA) between EU and NAFTA countries has been proposed; the Free Trade Area of the Americas, consisting of Canada, Mexico, and the United States, was endorsed in December 1994 by these countries' leaders, who participated in the Summit of the Americas; the summiteers of the Asia-Pacific Economic Cooperation (APEC) meeting in Bogor, Indonesia, in November 1994 established a goal of free and open trade and investment in the region by the year 2010 by developed countries and by the year 2020 by developing countries of the APEC; SAPTA, the South Asian Preferential Trade Agreement, has been initiated. Besides such regional arrangements, subregional (i.e., a contiguous area covering parts of several countries) development programs, such as the Tumen River Area Development program of Northeast Asia and the development program in the Singapore-Johore-Batan region of Southeast Asia, have been launched.

It is an open question whether regional arrangements represent WTO-plus, so to speak, by accelerating and extending on a nondiscriminatory basis the liberalization envisaged in the UR or whether they are likely to weaken the WTO by bypassing it. It is conceivable that with countries simultaneously being members of several such agreements, complex rules of origin will have to be devised to determine which trade flows get preferential treatment and to what extent. Such rules, by reducing the transparency and certainty of treatment, could impede the flows. Also, whether the many developing countries who are not yet members of any such regional arrangement should unilaterally liberalize on a nondiscriminatory basis rather than contemplate membership in one or more such arrangements is worth analyzing. The opportunities as well as threats posed by regionalism and subregionalism to a liberal global trading and investment order are explored in Chapter 7 and also in Chapter 12. The eight rounds of the MTN since 1947 have virtually eliminated all tariff and nontariff barriers to trade in most goods at national borders of industrialized countries, the exceptions being agriculture and some goods exported by developing countries, particularly textiles and apparel. Trade in textiles and apparel has been governed by the Multifibre Arrangement (MFA) of bilaterally negotiated (under the auspices of the GATT!) quotas. The UR agreement envisages the phaseout of MFA and reductions in tariffs on other manufactured exports of developing countries. Imports from developing countries accounted for roughly a third and an eighth, respectively, of total imports in the United States and the European Union (EU) in the early 1990s. These shares were roughly twice what they were in the 1970s. With the implementation of the UR agreement they are likely to increase even further. As a result, according to

Stephanie Flanders and Martin Wolf, "a spectre of irresistible competition from billions of impoverished workers disturbs industrialized countries" (*Financial Times*, July 24, 1995: 15). Whether increased imports from developing countries explain a significant part of the increased unemployment and decline in the real wages of unskilled workers in industrialized countries remains controversial. Yet at a political level, with the option of raising tariff and nontariff barriers at the border no longer feasible, the response in developed countries to increased import competition has been to demand "level" playing fields, with differences in domestic policies, particularly regulatory policies (e.g., environmental and labor standards and their enforcement), being viewed as creating or blunting international competitiveness.

In a world of increasing mobility of capital, differences among such domestic policies are also seen as creating policy-arbitrage opportunities with firms seeking to locate in countries with the most favorable policy regimes from their perspectives. The fear that firms might leave a country whose policies they perceive to be unfavorable could in turn induce countries to harmonize their policies, for example, by setting very lax environmental or labor standards. The prospect of such a "race to the bottom" in standards has led environmentalists to demand that standards be multilaterally set at sufficiently high levels and enforced through a denial of access to export markets for countries deviating from the set standards. However, the ministers who signed the Final Act of the UR were careful not to prejudge the issue in making their decisions relating to trade and the environment. Although acknowledging that measures necessary to protect the environment may conflict with the provisions of the Agreement on Trade in Services and desiring to coordinate the policies in the field of trade and environment without exceeding the competence of the multilateral trading system, they decided to establish the Committee on Trade and Environment in the WTO. In setting the terms of reference of the committee, the ministers were again cautious: They wanted the committee to identify the relationship between trade measures and environmental measures and to make appropriate recommendations on whether any modifications of the provisions of the multilateral trading system are required.

Since the Treaty of Versailles of 1919, which led to the establishment of the International Labor Organization (ILO), and even earlier, differences in labor standards among countries have been viewed as creating unfair competitive advantages. Repeated attempts have been made to link market access and the observance of labor standards in the GATT. Private arrangements among firms that actually or potentially restrict competition in a market have always been the domain of antimonopoly or antitrust policies within countries. Their absence or weak enforcement could disadvantage foreign firms in national markets. Indeed, this is one of the charges against Japan by the United States, and there are demands for harmonizing such competition policies. This is an issue of concern primarily to advanced industrialized countries. However, given the trend toward privatization of state monopolies in developing countries, it could become relevant to developing countries as well.

It is clear that the access of developing countries to the markets of developed countries, particularly in labor-intensive manufactures in which they have comparative advantage, will be threatened if the developed countries insist on setting and enforcing levels of labor or environmental standards beyond what such countries could afford at their stage of development. Besides, such threats to market access could lead to a very unfortunate slowdown or even reversal of the process of unilateral liberalization of foreign trade and payments regimes in many developing countries. Chapter 8 is devoted to the issues of the possible future linkage between trade policies on the one hand and environmental and labor standards on the other. I return to the developments since the signing of the UR on these issues in Chapter 12.

Even if there had been no pressure from developed countries to "level up" their domestic regulatory frameworks and institutions of economic management, developing countries would have had to reform their domestic financial as well as other institutions. For example, without an adequate legal system as it relates to commercial contracts, a framework for inviting and evaluating bids for public projects, and an efficient transport and telecommunications system, a developing country will find it difficult to integrate with the global economy and to derive maximum benefits from such integration. The post-UR environment is likely to be one of intense competition for markets for goods and for investment capital. The institutional reforms and innovations needed in developing countries to compete in such an environment are analyzed in Chapter 9.

Article III (paragraph 4) of the agreement establishing the WTO explicitly instructs the WTO to cooperate as appropriate with the IMF and the World Bank and affiliated agencies with a view to achieving greater coherence in global economic policymaking. The content and modalities of such cooperation were, however, left unspecified. At a minimum, there could be consultation among the agencies mentioned. At a maximum, there could be cross-conditionality in the sense of the benefits or rights of a country as a member of one agency being denied or reduced for that country's failing to meet its obligations to another agency of which it is a member. Given the dominance of the developed countries in the weighted voting system of decisionmaking of the IMF and World Bank, in contrast with WTO's one-member-one-vote majority decisionmaking, in the absence of a consensus, cross-conditionality may provide leverage to developed countries to pressure developing countries in the WTO. Problems could also arise if a country is a member of only a subset of those agencies. A speculative discussion of these issues is offered in Chapter 10. Chapter 11 summarizes the part of the book that was completed by the end of 1995 and offers some policy conclusions.

Chapter 12 takes up developments since 1995 and, in particular, the results of the first ministerial meeting of the WTO in Singapore during December 9–13, 1996.

Notes

1. UNCTAD has published six volumes of *International Monetary and Financial Issues for the 1990s*. Volume 6, published in 1995, deals with the implications of the UR for developing countries. This book was largely completed prior to the availability of Volume 6.

2 *The GATT, the ITO, and the WTO: Geneva 1947 to Marrakech 1994 through Havana 1947–1948*

The origin of the GATT can be traced to the U.S. government's *Proposals for the Expansion of World Trade and Employment* (hereafter, the *Proposals*), published on December 6, 1945, and forwarded to all other countries in the world. At the same time, the United States extended an invitation to fifteen countries (including Brazil, China, Cuba, and prepartition India, which then comprised contemporary Bangladesh, India, and Pakistan) to participate in negotiations for the reduction of tariffs and other barriers to trade. Fourteen countries with the notable exception of the Soviet Union accepted the U.S. invitation. In retrospect, nonacceptance by the Soviet Union should not be surprising. After all, it chose later not to become a member of the IMF and the World Bank even though it participated in the conference in Bretton Woods, New Hampshire, in 1944 that led to the establishment of the two institutions.

At the first meeting of the Economic and Social Council (ECOSOC) of the United Nations (UN) in 1946, the United States introduced a resolution calling for an international conference on trade and employment (which came to meet in Havana in November 1947) with the *Proposals* as its possible agenda. The resolution was unanimously adopted. ECOSOC appointed a preparatory committee for the conference consisting of the United States, Norway, Chile, Lebanon, and the fifteen countries invited by the United States for tariff-reduction negotiations. The Soviet Union again chose not to participate in the deliberations of the preparatory committee. In the meantime, the U.S. government also developed *Suggested Charter for an International Trade Organization* (hereafter, *Suggested Charter*) and circulated it to the preparatory committee, which accepted it as a basis for its deliberation.

India and the other developing countries in the preparatory committee viewed the *Proposals* and the *Suggested Charter* as serving the needs of industrial countries and as inimical to development (more on this in Chapter 3). The first meeting of the preparatory committee, except for adding a chapter on economic development, essentially adopted most of the U.S. draft, leaving it to a committee at UN headquarters in New York to complete and edit the text of the charter. The committee published its draft, known as the New York Draft, in January 1947.

On a motion by the United States, the preparatory committee also approved a memorandum on procedures to be followed in U.S.-initiated negotiations for tariff reductions. These negotiations took place at the second meeting of the committee in Geneva, where simultaneous discussion on the new draft of the charter as well as tariff negotiations went on. The talks on tariffs included, besides the eighteen participating members of the preparatory committee, Syria (as a member of a customs union with Lebanon) Burma, Ceylon, and Southern Rhodesia. The tariff bargaining proceeded on a product-by-product basis between pairs of countries, of which one was the principal supplier of each commodity for the other. In all, 123 bilateral negotiations covering 50,000 items took place in over 1,000 meetings and produced a single document called the General Agreement on Tariffs and Trade (GATT) on November 18, 1947. The twenty-three countries (now including Pakistan, which had since come to existence) participating in the tariff negotiations became the original contracting parties to this agreement.

The announcement of the completion of the GATT set the stage for the Havana conference, which opened on November 21, 1947. Fifty-six nations, again with the notable exception of the Soviet Union, participated in the conference. The most violent and protracted controversies at the conference were on development issues (see Chapter 3). These were resolved, after a prolonged deadlock, by a series of compromises. The Final Act, embodying the charter for the International Trade Organization (ITO), was signed on March 24, 1948, by fifty-three countries; Argentina and Poland refused to sign, and the authorization for Turkey's delegation to sign had been delayed in transmission.

As noted earlier, the tariff negotiations that led to the GATT and the discussions on a draft charter for the ITO proceeded simultaneously at the second meeting in Geneva of the preparatory committee for the Havana conference. The early draft of the GATT included clauses that implied an organization such as the ITO. However, the authority for negotiating tariff reduction, delegated by the U.S. Congress to the president, did not include the authority to negotiate an agreement to establish an international organization with the United States as a member. Thus these clauses had to be redrafted to eliminate any implication of an organization. The redrafted and eventually approved text explicitly stated that multilateral decisions under the GATT were to be taken by the

"CONTRACTING PARTIES" acting jointly and not by an organization.[1] The text, whenever it described any joint action by the contracting parties, referred to them in capital letters. Thus the GATT was to be only a multilateral agreement and not an organization. But it was designed to operate under the umbrella of the ITO once it came into being.

The ITO, however, never came into being, primarily because the United States did not ratify its charter. Although the president submitted the ITO charter to the Congress for approval in 1948, the wartime interest in designing postwar international institutions to resolve conflicts had waned by then. This and other factors, including the Republican Party gaining control of Congress with the presidency remaining with the Democratic Party, led the U.S. president to announce at the end of 1950 that he would no longer seek congressional approval for the ITO, thereby ending any prospect of its coming into being. The charter reflected the tenor of the times and included several features that allowed a lot of freedom for members to restrict imports (for example, in the event of significant unemployment). Since it is impossible to say whether it would have been amended to reflect changing realities and perceptions, one cannot categorically assert that its nonadoption was a blessing in disguise.

The GATT was completed in October 1947 before the approval of the ITO charter by the Havana conference in March 1948. Due to their fear that tariff reductions in the GATT might unravel if not implemented immediately, negotiators wished to bring the GATT into force before the ITO. As the negotiating authority delegated by the Congress for tariff reductions was to expire in mid-1948, the U.S. executive wanted to bring the GATT into force before that time without waiting until the ITO charter was ready. However, other countries preferred to put the GATT and the ITO charter simultaneously through their ratification procedures. A compromise between those who wished to implement the GATT without waiting for the ITO charter to be completed and those who preferred to wait was the adoption of the Protocol of Provisional Application, signed by the twenty-three contracting parties in October 1947.

The protocol called for the immediate application of the portion of Part I of the GATT relating to general most-favored-nation treatment and the schedule of tariff concessions offered by each contracting party and most of Part III, which dealt with procedural issues. Part II, containing twenty-one of the original thirty-five articles of the GATT and relating to the substantive obligations of the contracting parties, was to be implemented "to the fullest extent, not inconsistent with existing legislation" in each of the participating countries. These "existing legislation exceptions" to Part II obligations of the GATT enabled the parties to implement the GATT without having to repeal any existing legislation that might be inconsistent with Part II. Since the approval and ratification of the ITO charter were anticipated at the time, the provisional application of the GATT, with the exception relating to existing legislation, did not seem to be a major issue then. As it turned out, the ITO did not come into being and all subsequent attempts to ensure definitive, rather than provisional, application of the GATT never succeeded. The "existing legislation exceptions" became grandfather rights that continued to be invoked even in the late 1980s, according to Jackson (1990). The review session of the contracting parties in 1955 drafted a new protocol for an "Organization for Trade Cooperation," an organization far less elaborate than the ITO, and this too failed to win the approval of the U.S. Congress.

In Jackson's (1989: 89) words, "The GATT has limped along for nearly forty years with almost no 'basic constitution' designed to regulate its organizational activities and procedures." The only substantial formal amendment to the GATT was the 1965 protocol to add Part IV dealing with trade and development. Yet under GATT's auspices, eight successful rounds of MTNs for reducing barriers to trade have been concluded. What is more, for a quarter of a century after the GATT came to be provisionally applied until the first oil shock in 1973, world trade grew at an unprecedentedly high rate, at nearly 8 percent per year, and world output grew at 5 percent per year. After the first oil shock, the growth rate in both trade and output slowed to under 3 percent per year during 1974–1984. Growth of trade recovered to over 5 percent per year on an average during 1984–1994 and to 9.5 percent in 1994. During the period 1950–1994 as a whole, the volume of merchandise trade grew to nearly *fifteen* times its level in 1950, and output grew to somewhat under *six* times its level in 1950 (GATT, *International Trade: Trends and Statistics*, various issues up to 1995; and WTO 1995a). It is therefore tempting to conclude that in spite of all its structural faults, the GATT has enabled more rapid liberalization than otherwise would have happened and has substantially contributed to the growth of world trade and incomes since World War II and that with the establishment of the WTO, a formal organization that has the GATT framework of mediating international trade relations incorporated in it, the GATT will serve the future as well as it did the past. Such a conclusion is certainly plausible, indeed compelling, although a strict causal connection between the GATT and world growth in trade is impossible to establish.

In reassuring oneself of the potential of the WTO to promote future world trade and incomes, one has to be clear about the objectives and functions of institutions such as the GATT and the WTO. Certainly the rhetoric of global economic cooperation and of a fair and open multilateral trading system that promotes global welfare, rhetoric contained in the ministerial declaration establishing the WTO, should not be dismissed out of hand as empty. But one should realistically examine

whether the flaws, tensions, and conflicts that plagued the GATT's operation have been eliminated in the WTO architecture.

In analyzing the GATT as an international institutional framework, it is
useful to start with Jackson's (1990: 48) distinction between two models
of international institutions. One model is primarily of a forum for discussion and future negotiation that "has neither many concrete or precisely defined international rules or obligations nor a mechanism for implementing or enforcing such obligations." The second model is of an
institution with "concrete and precise rules which governments feel are
necessary" with "a mechanism for implementing or enforcing them."

The GATT, being a multilateral agreement with specified rules and
norms of behavior but without an explicit and strong mechanism for enforcing them, does not fit either model, although as Jackson points out, it
was gravitating toward the second. But aspects of the first model have
continued in the GATT. As Winham (1989: 51) notes, the GATT had become "an organization in which formal multilateral negotiation is a normal, but an exclusive means of conducting business. There is a natural
proclivity towards negotiation in this regime which tends to ensure that
any major problems facing the organization will sooner or later produce
a call for negotiation." Be that as it may, Jackson correctly suggests that
governments (and individuals) are not clear as to which model they prefer and that their rhetoric and actions are pointers to this ambivalence.
According to him, the U.S. government has been a strong advocate for
the need for improvements in the GATT dispute-settlement process and
in fact pushed for them in the UR negotiations. Yet at the same time, "in
practice the U.S. has been quite willing to attempt to subvert that process,
by a variety of procedural devices or simply by refusing to comply with
the results of the panel procedures which went against it" (Jackson 1990:
49). Indeed, even after succeeding in ensuring a much stronger (as compared with GATT) dispute-settlement mechanism in the WTO, the
United States ignored it and threatened to raise tariffs (which were
bound under GATT) on imports of luxury cars from Japan to punitively
high levels in order to increase its foreign share of Japan's auto-parts
market. The United States is by no means the only contracting party to
the GATT and member of the WTO that exhibits this contradiction between its rhetoric and practice. Yet it is too simplistic to infer from this
that GATT-WTO rules have no effect on the behavior of the parties (particularly the stronger ones). They abide by the rules when it suits them;
otherwise realpolitik takes over.

At a *fundamental level* GATT, and now the WTO, are no more than
frameworks "for a mediation of international trade relations, such that
conflicts about trade can be avoided and trade can take place in a stable
and predictable environment ... [and] for mutually beneficial coopera-

tive behavior, where the alternative was mutually destructive defensive behavior" (Low 1993: 20). But at a different level, Low sees the GATT also as a system of rules, the commitment to which could be used by governments to fend off domestic vested interests. Jackson (1990) cites instances in which congressional committees in the United States have taken considerable trouble to tailor legislative proposals to minimize the risk of a complaint to the GATT and instances when the Congress has been persuaded to drop GATT-inconsistent proposals. Indeed, even while threatening unilaterally to impose punitive tariffs on imports of luxury automobiles from Japan, the U.S. authorities stressed their commitment "to using the WTO to settle matters within the scope of the organization"; they stated they were "preparing a detailed case for submission" (WTO 1995b: 3). However, "at both the DSB [Dispute Settlement Body] and the CTG [Council on Trade in Goods], many members stressed that unilateral trade actions were contrary to WTO rules." The fact that the dispute was settled by the two parties after consultations requested by Japan as per WTO rules led the director-general of the WTO, Renato Ruggiero, to proclaim "the WTO dispute settlement has done its job as a deterrent against conflict and a promoter of agreement. The knowledge that both sides were prepared to use the system played a crucial role in pressing them towards a deal" (WTO 1995b: 3). A less self-interested observer would suggest that the WTO mattered, though how much it did would be impossible to determine. More skeptical observers would consider this episode more as one in which the WTO was a mere spectator and not a player.

Still, a reasonably strong case can be made that GATT-WTO rules, and the strengthened dispute-settlement mechanism of the WTO that sustains them, did in the past and will in the future influence behaviors even of the strong. This, of course, does not mean that the powerful among the members have abandoned what Jackson (1990) terms a "power-oriented approach," in which the relative power status of parties to any dispute determines the contours of its settlement, in favor of a "rules-oriented approach," in which the dispute is settled through a process and with reference to a set of rules to which both parties have previously agreed. Indeed, the U.S.-Japan auto-parts episode of 1995 is strong evidence that the power-oriented approach is alive and well!

In concluding this chapter, I feel it is worth examining how far the "flaws" of the GATT have been rectified in the WTO. Again, Jackson's (1990: sec. 5.1) comprehensive list of flaws provides a convenient starting point. First, with the establishment of the WTO as a formal organization, the perceived weakness of the GATT as the provisional application of a multilateral agreement with grandfather rights has been removed. Second, perhaps because of the difficulty in putting together the required majority to pass an amendment, GATT's amendment procedure was used rarely, and instead of amending the relevant articles, leaders negotiated an elaborate system of plurilateral side agreements and codes (such as those on antidumping and others of the Tokyo Round). The membership of the stand-alone side agreements and codes differed, and each had its own dispute-settlement procedures. This flaw has been addressed by a clearer amendment procedure (Article X) and by bringing in all *multilateral* trade agreements as integral parts of the agreement on establishing the WTO and making them binding on *all* members of the WTO. Except for the plurilateral agreement on government procurement, other remaining agreements relating to bovine meat, civil aircraft, and dairy, although they address issues covered by the WTO, are binding on those members of the WTO accepting them and create no obligations or rights for those members not accepting them. Third, the relationship between the GATT and the domestic laws of contracting parties varied. In many countries international agreements entered into by them *automatically* become parts of domestic law. In others, such as the United States, unless the relevant GATT rules are incorporated into domestic law by legislation, domestic laws override a GATT rule if the application of the latter conflicts with the former. It does not appear that in agreeing to the establishment of the WTO, the latter countries have also agreed to take steps to integrate the WTO formally into their own domestic law. Thus the relationship of the WTO to domestic laws is likely to remain as varied as that of the GATT to such laws.

Fourth, articles of the WTO relating to its original membership (Article XI), accession of new members (Article XII), and ministerial decisions on acceptance and accession to the agreement establishing the WTO have expanded on the corresponding articles of the GATT. But unfortunately, Article XIII of the WTO incorporates the "one-time opt-out" feature of Article XXXV of the GATT. Thus the provisions of multilateral trade agreements, subsumed under the WTO, "shall not apply as between any Member and any other Member if either of the Members at the time the other becomes a Member, does not consent to such application" (*GATT* 1994a: 15). However, original members of the WTO (i.e., contracting parties to the GATT 1947) cannot invoke this provision unless they also did so earlier under Article XXXV of the GATT. A famous (or notorious depending upon one's point of view) instance of the invoking of Article XXXV was when fourteen countries, including all the major industrialized countries, invoked it against Japan at the time of its accession in 1955. Dam (1970: 340) comments that "this massive decision to discriminate was motivated largely by a fear of low-wage competition in manufactured goods, although fear of unfair competition and political factors also played a part." China, a low-wage economy whose exports of labor-

intensive manufactures have grown rapidly, was rebuffed in its attempt
to gain entry to the WTO as a founder member. As of April 1997, its accession was still to be settled. "WTO members are pressing China to open
its economy further to foreign participation and are demanding Beijing
to agree to a time table for market liberalization, including undertakings
on opening its service sector" (*Financial Times*, April 22, 1997: 8). Even if
China is allowed to enter the WTO, Article IX of the WTO could be invoked against it at the time of entry.

Also, there are indications that *domestic* regulatory policies (such as
those relating to market structure) are becoming subjects of international
negotiations, not an altogether positive development. According to
Hoekman (1995: 8), in discussions of their accession with transition
economies, existing GATT members (who are automatically entitled to
become members of WTO) are

> seeking assurances that substantial progress will have been achieved to-
> wards privatizing production units and establishing a market-based regula-
> tory environment. Contestability of markets is reportedly being demanded
> in the case of China, involving the removal of exclusive privileges or aboli-
> tion of monopolies. This is an interesting development, insofar as neither the
> GATT or the WTO prejudges market structures or the form of ownership of
> enterprises.

Of course, domestic reforms and increasing competition in China or
elsewhere in the developing world are desirable. But the use of admis-
sion to the WTO as a lever to achieve these outcomes when no such demands are made on existing members seems unfair. China has, in any
case, announced, following the November 1995 meeting of the Asia-Pacific Economic Cooperation (APEC) forum in Osaka, that it would reduce
tariffs on a list of 4,000 imported items, though it has not in fact done so.
According to a report in the *Financial Times* (December 7, 1995: 4), China
has been provided with a U.S.-drafted "road map" laying out the terms
for China's entry into the WTO, and the Osaka announcement was a
down payment aimed at improving the climate for China's negotiations
with a WTO working party. Another report in the same day's *Financial
Times* said that negotiations of the WTO working party with Russia were
progressing, but Russia's entry remains some way off, possibly occurring
at the end of the 1990s.

Fifth, ambiguities surrounding the power of the contracting parties of
the GATT, and the fact that its council has been created by a resolution of
the contracting parties with no treaty status, have been resolved in Article IV of the WTO, which relates to the WTO's structure; under this article, a ministerial conference of representatives of all the members is the
decisionmaking body. The conference is required to meet at least once

every two years. The first conference met in Singapore in December 1996. The article authorizes a general council (composed of representatives of all the members to carry out the functions of the ministerial conference between its meetings) and also establishes several other councils and committees.

Sixth, the dispute-settlement mechanism (DSM) of the WTO is much stronger than that of the GATT. As summarized by Schott (1994: 125), in the GATT there were many delays between the establishment of panels on disputes to the conclusion of their proceedings; the parties to the dispute could block the acceptance of the panel reports by the GATT General Council, since acceptance required consensus; and finally, even if the panel findings were approved by the council and it authorized retaliation against a contracting party not complying with the rulings of a panel, whether there was compliance or retaliation in the case of noncompliance could depend on the relative strengths of the disputants. For example, the Netherlands complained against the import quotas imposed by the United States on its dairy products. For seven years in a row from 1953, the contracting parties authorized the Netherlands to impose restraints on its imports of U.S. grains. Although the United States did not remove the dairy import quotas, the Netherlands chose not to retaliate as authorized (Jackson 1990: 63–64). Stated somewhat differently, the means of enforcement of any panel decision was basically the threat of retaliation by the complainant and possibly other contracting parties. Clearly such a threat by small countries would not be credible, let alone be in their interests. However, if a number of small countries band together to complain against powerful members and the panel rules in their favor, a joint retaliation threat by them could be more credible. The WTO procedures for multiple complainants allow for this possibility.

Jackson's analysis of the dispute-settlement procedures of the GATT during 1947–1986 suggests, somewhat surprisingly but happily, that the compliance record of the GATT panel recommendations was very respectable and the developing countries fared well. In only 8 to 10 of 117 cases for which information was available was there noncompliance. Besides, of the 233 cases filed with the GATT, 205 were against industrial countries, and of these, 155 were instituted by other industrial countries. Thus the GATT mechanism did not fare too badly. Under the WTO's mechanism, panels have to be established expeditiously and strict time deadlines are set for various stages of the panel proceedings. Instead of requiring, as the GATT did, a consensus to *adopt* a panel report, under the WTO, consensus is required to *block* a report. A body to which an appeal can be made against panel findings is also part of the mechanism. Automatic authority to retaliate (including retaliation in a different sector) against noncompliance is also provided. Thus the WTO mechanism is much stronger than the GATT one. But as in all such international mechanisms, the operation of the WTO's DSM will have to contend with power realities, as is already evident from the recent (1995) episode relating to the U.S.-Japan auto-parts dispute. I return to issues relating to the DSM in Chapters 6 and 12.

Last, the GATT was originally intended to be subsumed under the ITO, which was to have been the third of the international organizations (the other two being the IMF and the World Bank) governing the whole gamut of international economic transactions. With the ITO not coming into being, GATT's relationship with the IMF and the World Bank was not made explicit except for Article XV; this article relates to exchange-rate arrangements and required the GATT to seek the cooperation of the IMF. In contrast, the WTO (Article III, paragraph 5) explicitly calls for cooperation of the WTO with the IMF and the World Bank. A cooperation agreement between the two institutions was signed in December 1996, and a similar agreement with the World Bank and the WTO is being finalized. Interestingly, although the *financial institutions* (IMF and the World Bank) are mentioned, there is no mention of UNCTAD, a *trade institution* in the WTO charter![2]

It should be evident from the previous discussion that some of the more serious shortcomings of the GATT, many of which arose from its unfortunate history, have been rectified in the charter of the WTO. Still, the WTO, as the GATT did, allows its members to opt out of or temporarily suspend their obligations of membership under specified, presumably exceptional, circumstances. Nonetheless, with the WTO in place, the chances of members using a rule-based rather than a power-based approach to international economic relations have improved.

Notes

In writing this chapter, I have very heavily drawn on Dam (1970), Jackson (1989, 1990), and particularly Wilcox (1949).

1. A contracting party need not necessarily be a sovereign nation; it can be a distinct customs area, such as Hong Kong, a British crown colony until mid-1997.

2. However, in his annual report (WTO 1995c: 10) the director-general of WTO states that the WTO secretariat and UNCTAD are cooperating in "a results-oriented initiative to help African countries expand and diversify their trade" and that "further cooperation between the WTO and UNCTAD will not be limited to the WTO program of activities for Africa. To enhance cooperation between the two organizations and develop further the already strong complementarity, the Secretary-General of UNCTAD and I have agreed (i) to hold meetings, chaired jointly by us, every six months beginning in mid-January 1996; (ii) to improve the working relationship between the two organizations at all levels, in such areas as research, trade and investment, trade and competition, trade and the environ-

ment, and trade and development." The Singapore ministerial declaration envisages the WTO drawing upon ongoing studies in UNCTAD with respect to investment. The ministers, in adopting a plan of action to assist least-developed countries, agreed to organize a WTO meeting with UNCTAD and the International Trade Center as soon as possible in 1997 (WTO 1997: 2–3).

3 Developing Countries and the GATT: Havana 1947–1948 to Tokyo 1979

Among the original twenty-three contracting parties to the GATT in 1947, eleven (or thirteen if the Czechoslovak Republic and the Union of South Africa are included) were developing countries.[1] The preparatory committee to the Havana conference, which drew up the draft charter for the ITO, consisted of eighteen of those twenty-three, including six (or eight if again the Czechoslovak Republic and South Africa are included) developing countries.

As mentioned in Chapter 2, in December 1945, the United States had circulated its *Proposals for the Expansion of World Trade and Employment* to all countries of the world and had invited fifteen of the eighteen (excluding Chile, Lebanon, and Norway) to participate in negotiations for the reduction of tariffs and other barriers to trade. These fifteen later became the preparatory committee for negotiating the mutual reduction of tariffs. Brazil, Cuba, and India, which were among the fifteen, and other developing countries viewed the *Proposals* as motivated by a desire on the part of developed countries to keep them in dependence. India deemed the imposition of direct controls on foreign trade necessary for promoting rapid and large-scale industrialization. Wilcox (1949) attributes to Latin American countries views he considers even more extreme. It is worth reproducing in full his description of Latin American views, since some of them, in a different and perhaps less extreme form, reappeared in the demands in the UN for a new international economic order in the 1970s. He claims that Latin Americans argued that

> wealth and income . . . should be redistributed between the richer and the poor states. Upon the rich obligations should be imposed; upon the poor, privileges should be conferred. The former should recognize it as their duty to export capital for the development of backward areas; the latter should not be

expected to insure the security of such capital, once it was obtained. The former should reduce barriers to imports; the latter should be left free to increase them. The former should sell manufactured goods below price ceilings; the latter should sell raw materials and food stuffs above price floors. Immediate requirements should be given precedence over long-run policies, development over reconstruction, and the interests of regionalism over world economy. Freedom of action, in the regulation of trade, must be preserved. The voluntary acceptance by all states, of equal obligations with respect to commercial policy must be rejected as an impairment of sovereignty and a means by which the strong would dominate the weak. (Wilcox 1949: 32)

It is interesting that some of these demands were conceded later and became part of the GATT under the so-called enabling clause, which emerged from the Tokyo Round. This clause required that developing countries be provided a "differential and more favorable treatment" and be excused from having to reciprocate regarding the concessions and commitments undertaken by developed countries.

It was noted earlier that the draft charter for the ITO drawn up by the preparatory committee for the Havana conference was almost unanimously denounced by the developing countries at the conference for being against their interests.[2] Many of the demands attributed by Wilcox to Latin American developing countries were in fact advanced by them at the conference. Indeed, according to Wilcox, a proposal was made at the conference that if a loan application to the World Bank was turned down, a new one should be supported by the ITO and that an autonomous economic development commission should be established within the ITO.

Actually, in the chapter on economic development that was included in the ITO's final charter, the ITO was assigned only a promotional and advisory role; it could not itself finance, construct, or operate developmental projects. It was presumed that resources (except for lumpy, large-scale investment in infrastructure) for development, particularly capital, would normally be obtained from private sources. The World Bank was to assist in building infrastructure. The article that dealt with foreign investment allowed a member "to take any appropriate safeguards necessary to ensure that foreign investment is not used as a basis for interference in internal affairs or national policies" and "to determine whether and to what extent and upon what terms it will allow future foreign investment." With respect to such investment, a member was obligated merely to give "due regard . . . to the desirability of avoiding discrimination as between foreign investments" and to provide "adequate security for existing and future investments" (Wilcox 1949: 236–237). It is clear that these articles are not exactly welcoming of foreign investment. Until the UR agreement on trade-related investment measures, investment issues were not addressed in any rounds of the MTN.

Wilcox (1949: 148) points out that more than three-fourths of the economic development chapter of the ITO charter consisting of Articles 13 and 15 "is devoted to an elaboration of methods by which underdeveloped countries may obtain release from commitments assumed in trade agreements and under the charter with respect to commercial policy." These commitments from which release may be sought covered (1) bound tariffs, (2) nonuse of quantitative restrictions on imports, and (3) noncreation of new trade preferences. Thus without securing such a release from the ITO or other trading partners affected, a developing country could not use any method forbidden by the charter or by a trade agreement. The release from commitments is not absolute in the sense that the use of methods otherwise prohibited is subject to conditions prescribed in the charter itself and limited in time. For this reason, the provisions of the chapter on economic development were considered completely inadequate and onerous by the developing countries; most of them then (until the 1980s) viewed industrialization through import substitution behind high barriers as the only path to development.

The ITO charter contained the chapter "Intergovernmental Commodity Agreements," which was of interest to developing countries. Wilcox (1949) notes that such agreements permit the adoption of trade-restraining measures in the case of primary commodities, measures that are prohibited by the charter in the case of manufactured commodities. This inconsistency of treatment was justified in the charter with the assertion that "the conditions under which some primary commodities are produced, exchanged and consumed . . . may, at times, necessitate special treatment of the international trade in such commodities through intergovernmental agreement" (Wilcox 1949: 120). The now familiar arguments that such agreements promote an orderly and rapid adjustment between production and consumption that would not be brought about by market forces alone and that they promote stability of the market on the basis of prices that are remunerative to producers and fair to consumers are spelled out in the chapter, which also provides for the administration of commodities trade under agreements by separate commodity councils. Wilcox (1949: 124) records the possibility of the abuse of such agreements and wryly comments that the chapter drew "fire both from the right and from the left. Those who oppose all commodity agreements believe that it compromises with evil; that government cartels should be outlawed along with private cartels. Those who seek the creation of a large number of such agreements complain that its requirements will make them difficult to get"! A demand by developing countries for the stabilization of commodity prices through the creation and operation of buffer stocks was an essential part of the demand for a new international economic order in the 1970s.

With ITO's demise and until the adoption of Part IV on trade and development in 1964, Article XVIII, dealing with governmental assistance to economic development, itself a carryover of Article 13 of the chapter on economic development in the ITO charter, was the principal provision in the GATT dealing with trade problems of developing countries. The GATT contains only a passing reference to commodity agreements in its Article XX, which deals with general exceptions to the obligations of contracting parties. Dam (1970) points out that even after its extensive revisions in 1955, Article XVIII retained its essentially passive legislative approach to trade problems, typical of the early GATT, and reflected that import substitution was a preferred strategy of development. In any case, given the consultations and annual reporting requirements and reviews needed for taking advantage of most sections of Article XVIII for imposing trade-restricting measures for any extended period of time, few developing countries made major use of it. Instead they availed themselves of its provision under Section B that allowed the use of quantitative restrictions (QRs) for containing balance-of-payments deficits.

In 1958, a decade after the conclusion of the GATT, a panel of experts (Gottfried Haberler, James Meade, Jan Tinbergen, and Oswaldo Campos) appointed by the GATT with Haberler as chairman published its report. After thoroughly examining the trade relations between less developed and developed countries, it came to the conclusion that barriers of all kinds in developed countries to the import of products from developing countries contributed significantly to the trade problems of developing countries. The GATT responded to the Haberler report by establishing the so-called Committee III, which was to review the trade measures restricting less-developed-country exports and to recommend a program for trade expansion by reducing trade barriers. The response of developed countries to Committee III reports, although positive, did not result in substantial reductions in barriers. Indeed, some of the barriers identified by Committee III, such as significant tariffs on tropical products, tariff escalation, quantitative restrictions, and internal taxes continued to exist nearly three decades later at the start of UR negotiations. The disappointment with this outcome led twenty-one developing countries to introduce a resolution in the GATT in 1963 calling for an action program consisting of a standstill on all new tariff and nontariff barriers, elimination within two years of all GATT-illegal quantitative restrictions, removal of all duties on tropical primary products, elimination of internal taxes on products wholly or mainly produced in developing countries, and adoption of a schedule for reduction and elimination of tariffs on semiprocessed and processed products. Some elements of this action program were still among the demands of developing countries twenty years later at the 1982 GATT ministerial meeting. It is interesting, if not ironic, that yet another action plan, this time for least-developed countries, is included in WTO's Singapore ministerial declaration of December 1996. It also includes a provision for duty-free access to world markets for such countries (WTO 1997: 9).

The GATT ministerial meeting of 1963, in response to the demand for an action program, appointed a committee to draft amendments to the GATT to provide a legal and institutional framework within which the GATT contracting parties could discharge their responsibilities toward developing countries. Dam (1970) remarks that this step was also a reaction to the preparations already in progress for the first UNCTAD. The proposed amendments were approved in 1964 and became Part IV of the GATT, entitled "Trade and Development." He concludes that apart from its symbolic importance in sensitizing the contracting parties to the new role of the GATT in development, less-developed countries achieved little by way of precise commitments (and even these were highly qualified) but a lot in terms of verbiage. Among the major provisions of Part IV is that on reciprocity (or more precisely, nonreciprocity): The developed countries decided not to require reciprocity for their commitments to reduce tariff and other barriers from developing countries. This provision, far from being introduced for the first time in Part IV, had in fact been included in the principles for negotiations set forth by the ministerial meeting that launched the Kennedy Round of the MTNs (Dam 1970). Besides, the European Community (EC) had announced that it would not expect reciprocity from developing countries as early as the Dillon Round. In retrospect, far from benefiting developing countries, this provision actually placed them in a weaker position to combat GATT-inconsistent barriers in developed countries against their exports.

After the incorporation of Part IV in 1964, the next major GATT event from the perspective of developing countries was the grant of a ten-year waiver from the most-favored-nation (MFN) clause with respect to tariff and other preferences favoring the trade of developing countries. This so-called Generalized System of Preferences (GSP) was later included under the rubric of the enabling clause of the Tokyo Round, which formulated the "differential and more favorable treatment" of developing countries in the GATT. Under GSP each developed country could choose the countries to be favored, the commodities to be covered, the extent of tariff preferences, and the period for which the preferences were granted. In fact, some countries (the United States and the European Community) linked the granting of preferences to the performance of a developing country in nontrade-related areas. For example, the United States withdrew GSP status from Chile in 1987 because Chile did not afford its workers "internationally accepted" rights. Besides, some of the more advanced developing countries benefited to a greater extent from GSP, leading to the demand from developed countries for the "graduation" of such countries from the ranks of those entitled to GSP. Again, as was the case with reciprocity, the benefits, if any, from GSP to developing countries were far outweighed by the cost in terms of weakening their case against other GATT-inconsistent barriers in developed countries to their exports.

Under the leadership of UNCTAD's first secretary-general, Raul Prebisch, developing countries, seventy-five in all, formed a solid bloc in its first meeting (UNCTAD I) in 1964 and voted nearly unanimously for recommendations that espoused a managed international market and discriminatory trade arrangements as the best means to close the "foreign exchange gap" (i.e., the difference between their export earnings and import requirements for sustaining their growth targets). The developed countries were divided with the French in particular and the EC in general offering some support to the positions of developing countries; others, led by the United States, opposed them (the conversion of the United States to ideas of "managed trade" with respect to its own trade with Japan came thirty years later!). Since the developed countries were the ones that were to take the actions recommended by UNCTAD I and they were opposed, not much action took place. Of course, as noted earlier, the GATT responded to UNCTAD I with its Part IV on trade and development. UNCTAD II in 1968 accomplished little except to pass more fruitless resolutions (Dam 1970: ch. 21).

The solidarity of developing countries was at its height, according to Haggard (1995), during the period 1965–1980, or roughly from UNCTAD I (1964) to the conclusion of GATT's Tokyo Round of the MTNs in 1979. According to him, this was also the period when the pace of accession to the GATT by developing countries slowed with only twelve countries becoming contracting parties. In fact, the number of developing countries in the GATT grew by thirty-five from the original nine at the end of 1949 to forty-four by 1965. But most of the thirty-five were automatically admitted under Article XXVI(5c), being sponsored by their former colonial powers. However, many of these apparently did not take an active part in the Dillon and Kennedy Rounds of the MTNs in the 1960s, since the total number of countries participating in them were, respectively, forty-five and forty-eight (Jackson 1990: Table 3). In the Tokyo Round the total number of participants rose to ninety-nine, and the developing countries not only took an active part but also were united in their positions on many issues. As noted earlier, the enabling clause of differential and more favorable treatment of developing countries was an outcome of the Tokyo Round. However, to prevent their access of benefits under GATT's MFN clause without having to reciprocate, many of the agreements of the Tokyo Round relating to nontariff barriers were in the form of side agreements or codes. The privileges and obligations of the codes were available only to those contracting parties of the GATT who chose to sign the codes.

Although the privileges of most codes tended to be applied on an MFN basis for all signatories, there was a notable exception in the case of the code for subsidies. Jackson (1989: 60) calls attention to the fact that the U.S. statute implementing the subsidies code was phrased in a way that the executive branch could deem that the signing by a developing country would not in itself be sufficient to persuade the United States to extend to that country the privileges of the code. For a country to get the full benefit of the code, the United States required, in addition to its signing the code, a separate bilateral commitment by that country to undertake a level of discipline on subsidies beyond what is called for in the code. India challenged the United States on this issue in 1980, and a GATT panel was established. But before the panel made any determination, the dispute was settled by the two parties.

The Tokyo Round, the first round of the MTNs in which the developing countries participated in strength and with cohesion, produced outcomes that were not in their long-term interests, primarily because their demands continued to be driven by the import-substitution ideology. The formal incorporation at the Tokyo Round of their demands for a differential and more favorable treatment, including not being required to reciprocate regarding any tariff "concessions" by the developed countries, triply hurt them: once through the direct costs of enabling them to continue their import-substitution strategies, a second time by allowing the developed countries to get away with their own GATT-inconsistent barriers (i.e., in textiles) against import from developing countries, and a third time by allowing the industrialized countries to keep higher-than-average MFN tariffs on goods of export interest to developing countries.

The 1980s saw the accession of twenty-five more developing countries, including some middle-income countries, into the GATT. In the first half of this decade, that is, the period leading up to the launching of the Uruguay Round in 1986, the earlier solidarity of the developing countries began to erode for several reasons. First, the faith in the strategy of import-substituting industrialization, which had prompted the solidarity, itself eroded in some major developing countries. Second was the onset of the debt crisis of the early 1980s. Third, and most important, the results from several research studies published in the late 1970s and early 1980s on the high cost of import substitution and inward orientation and the outstanding success of East Asian countries as well as Chile with their outward orientation began to sink in. Some developing countries began to liberalize their regimes unilaterally. But by no means was there any consensus among developing countries about the necessity of outward orientation and of liberalization of foreign trade in goods, services, and foreign investment, as the prenegotiation process of the Uruguay Round was to amply demonstrate.

The experience of developing countries in the GATT up to the conclusion of the Tokyo Round could be interpreted in two diametrically opposed ways. On the one hand, it could be said that from the Havana conference on, the developing countries have been repeatedly frustrated in getting the GATT to reflect their concerns. Tariffs and other barriers in industrialized countries on their exports were reduced to a smaller extent than those on exports of developed countries in each round of the MTNs. Products in which they had a comparative advantage, such as textiles and apparel, were taken out of the GATT disciplines altogether. Agriculture, a sector of great interest to developing countries, largely remained outside the GATT framework. "Concessions" granted to developing countries, such as the inclusion of Part IV on trade and development and the Tokyo Round enabling clause on special and differential treatment, were mostly rhetorical, and others, such as GSP, were always heavily qualified and quantitatively small. In sum, the GATT was unfriendly, if not actively hostile, to the interests of developing countries.

The other interpretation is that the developing countries, in their relentless but misguided pursuit of the import-substitution strategy of development, in effect opted out of the GATT. Instead of demanding and receiving crumbs from the rich man's table, such as GSP and a permanent status of inferiority under the "special and differential" treatment clause, had they participated fully, vigorously, and on equal terms with the developed countries in the GATT and had they adopted an outward-oriented development strategy, they could have achieved far faster and better growth. The success of East Asia suggests that the second interpretation is closer to the truth.

Notes

1. A classic study of developing countries in the GATT legal framework is Hudec (1987).

2. Although trade issues were excluded from the Bretton Woods Conference of 1944, there had been considerable work relating to ITO prior to 1944, the most important by Keynes. In his memorandum of 1942, he suggested commodity price stabilization and the financing of international buffer stocks as major functions of an international trade organization. According to Hans Singer, Keynes and other participants of the Bretton Woods conference firmly believed that ITO would be established. I owe these remarks to Bernhard Gunter.

4 The GATT: A Negotiating History Between Tokyo 1979 and Marrakech 1994

The Tokyo Round agreement and codes left many problems unresolved, including trade in agriculture, the inconsistency of the Multifibre Arrangement for trade in textiles with GATT principles (although it was accepted by the contracting parties despite the inconsistency), and safeguards issues (particularly the increasing use of discriminatory gray-area measures such as voluntary export restraints). Also, developed countries became increasingly dissatisfied with nonreciprocity and differential and more favorable treatment as they applied to the more successful developing countries. Further, with the perceived comparative advantage of industrialized countries shifting away from manufactured goods to services (particularly high-tech services), the United States took the initiative, with support later from other industrialized countries, to explore the possibility of a new round of MTNs on "new" issues such as trade in services, trade-related intellectual property, and investment. Another major factor that motivated the United States was the growing protectionist sentiment in the U.S. Congress as U.S. trade deficits grew. The Reagan administration sought to counter congressional action that was bound to be protectionist with the promise of multilateral negotiations. Although interested in bringing trade in agriculture and textiles into the same set of GATT rules that governed trade in manufactured goods, the developing countries were not enthusiastic about negotiating "new" issues.

The GATT ministerial meeting of 1982 was called to examine the functioning of the multilateral system. The preparatory committee for the meeting had compiled a long list of around thirty separate items for consideration by the ministers. Low (1993: 191) comments that its length, and the suddenness with which it grew, were extraordinary developments in the GATT context. Until the Tokyo Round, not much consideration had been given to anything but tariffs, and even in the Tokyo Round, except for the government procurement code, other issues were in any case elaborations of existing GATT provisions. The list grew in part because the contracting parties felt free to add issues concerning their own parochial interests.

Although the United States would have liked the meeting to be the first step toward a new round of MTNs, it did not attract much support at the meeting. A group of developing countries led by Brazil and India, two of the most influential countries in the GATT, was strongly opposed on the grounds that the developing countries were not ready to negotiate on services on an equal footing with the developed countries, and besides, the developed countries had not lived up to their obligations in the case of trade in textiles and agricultural products. They demanded commitments from developed countries not to introduce any new GATT-inconsistent measures (the so-called stand-still demand) and to remove any such measures in existence (the "roll back" demand). The drafting of a ministerial declaration at the conclusion of the meeting proved contentious.

The final text that emerged at the end of five days of the meeting (two days beyond its scheduled closing) was not a consensus document. Australia dissociated itself from it, and the EC issued an interpretive statement that in effect distanced it from any commitment to new negotiations or obligations in relation to agricultural products. With respect to the stand-still and roll-back demands, the final text was ambiguous regarding whether there was a firm commitment or merely a statement of intentions and an undertaking of "best efforts." The EC made explicit that it read the text to mean only that best efforts would be deployed. The operational part of the final text enunciated a two-year work program for the GATT (until its next ministerial meeting in 1984) involving seventeen topics: safeguards, rules and activities relating to developing countries, dispute-settlement procedures, trade in agriculture (with a committee on trade in agriculture to carry out this part of the work program), tropical products, quantitative restrictions and other nontariff measures, tariff escalation, review of the operation of multilateral trade agreements and arrangements, structural adjustment and trade policy, trade in counterfeit goods, export of domestically prohibited goods, export credit for capital goods, textiles and clothing, problems of trade in certain natural resource products, exchange-rate fluctuations and their effect on trade, dual pricing and rules of origin, and services (Low 1993: ch. 9).

Even before the work program was completed, Prime Minister Nakasone of Japan broached the idea of a new round of MTNs in 1983, and the leaders of seven industrialized countries (the so-called G-7) in their meeting in 1984 agreed to consult among their trading partners about the objectives and timing of a new round. However, there was by then no change in the opposition of major developing countries, and the EC's reservations had not dissipated either. Informal discussions in the GATT on a new round began in early 1985. In May 1985, the EC called for a meeting of high officials to consider issues involved in launching it. According to Low (1993: ch. 9), after a bitter and contentious debate during summer 1985, the United States took the hitherto unusual step of calling for a vote rather than arriving at a consensus and won. A special meeting of the contracting parties was called in October 1985, and they agreed that the preparatory process for a new round was already on and appointed a group of senior officials to further the process. But this group found it difficult to come to an agreement on the terms of its report to the contracting parties given the firm opposition of key developing countries. Yet before the contracting parties met in November 1985, the EC, Brazil, and India had already agreed informally to start the new round. The parties, when they met, decided to establish a formal preparatory committee to put together a set of recommendations by mid-July 1986 for adoption at the ministerial meeting at Punta del Este in Uruguay in September 1986.

The preparatory committee ran into many of the same conflicts as the group of senior officials. The topics before the committee had expanded from the seventeen in the work program of 1982 to thirty-one, of which only nineteen eventually became the subject of specific negotiating mandates and four came to be mentioned in the preamble to the ministerial declaration launching the UR. Apart from the committee, individual countries and overlapping groups of countries began to circulate draft texts for the ministerial declaration. These included Australia; Canada; Japan; the Group of Nine (GN), consisting of Australia, Canada, New Zealand, and members of the European Free Trade Area; and the Group of Ten (GT) developing countries, led by Brazil and India and also including Argentina, Cuba, Egypt, Nicaragua, Nigeria, Peru, Tanzania, and Yugoslavia. Whereas the GN was clear about the need for launching a new round, the GT was not convinced. In the event, the GT did not attract more members and presented a minority text to the preparatory committee. In contrast, the GN was able to attract a group of twenty developing countries to meet with it. Eventually, the GN came to include them and other major industrialized countries, growing to a membership of forty countries. This group of forty, or GF, chaired by Colombia and Switzerland, presented the majority text. Argentina on its own presented a third text (Low 1993: ch. 10).

Winham (1989) provides a fascinating description of the drama of the Punta del Este ministerial meeting. Without a single agreed-upon text from the preparatory committee, the meeting began with three texts, but the main contention was between the GT and GF texts. The former reflected the resistance of some developing countries to the U.S. demand to include new issues: services, intellectual property, and investment measures. But the GT position eroded, and a growing consensus emerged around the U.S. position once the United States in effect gave an ultimatum that it would withdraw from the conference altogether if these issues were not included. The EC did not fully accept the position of the GF text on agriculture. In spite of the creative effort of the chairman, Enrique Iglesias, minister of foreign affairs of Uruguay, who formed a "little plenary" consisting of the leading minister and one deputy from each country to discuss the texts, not all problems could be solved. After three days of meetings, no agreements had been reached on any subject. The chairman then created a small consultation committee of twenty nations representing the contending positions at the meeting; its membership was by invitation only. In addition, two substantive groups on services and agriculture were established to work simultaneously with the consultation committee. The chairman on his own initiative decided to treat the GF text as the basis for discussion in the consultation committee over the protests of those developing countries supporting the GT text. But he allowed amendments to the GF text that in turn drew protests from developed countries. Thirty-one amendments were initially offered and reduced to fourteen subsequently.

When the consultation committee met for the last time, at 6:00 P.M. the day before the ministerial meeting was scheduled to end, nothing substantial had been decided. With the U.S. delegation announcing with great fanfare that it would depart for the United States the next morning with or without a final declaration and threatening to call a vote in the committee rather than achieve a consensus, other members of the committee felt pressured to come to an agreement. By midnight, once India and the United States had come to an agreement that the negotiation on services would be undertaken separately, other disputed issues such as trade-related intellectual property and investment measures were quickly settled. In agriculture, agreement was reached at 2:00 A.M., and by 4:30 A.M. the fourteen amendments to the GF text had been discussed and withdrawn except for a statement that was included in the objectives section of the final text and that called on nations to link actions on trade liberalization with efforts to improve the functioning of the international monetary system. The draft agreed to by the consultation committee was approved by the full plenary by midday.

The analysis of Winham of the Punta del Este session and the entire UR prenegotiation process is worth reproducing, since it has some extremely pertinent lessons for the future functioning of the WTO. He concluded that the process

> succeeded in the end because of the widely held perception that failure to begin a new negotiation would have harmful consequences for the GATT regime and for the prospects for continued liberalization of international

trade. Thus, crisis avoidance was an important motivation during both the early prenegotiation period and the Punta-del-Este session. However, once the momentum in favor of a new negotiation had developed, the main motivation behind each delegation's activities became even more sharply focussed as a fear of being isolated and blamed for the failure of the special session. For example, most of the G-10 [i.e., GT] developing countries abandoned their hard-line opposition to a services negotiation during the Punta del Este session, until only India and an increasingly uncertain Brazil were left. In the end, India found it impolitic to be isolated and it acquiesced. The same explanation accounts for the eleventh hour acceptance by the French of a negotiation on agriculture. The actions of these countries, as well as others that withdrew amendments to the draft declaration, point up that even in a consensual regime majority rule still exercises a profound influence over political behavior. What is avoided in consensual regimes are narrow votes to break deadlocks, which means that action is more difficult to achieve than in democratic regimes which operate on the basis of formal majority rule. However, the special session demonstrated that the will of a large majority can be ultimately persuasive in a consensual organization even in the face of a powerful and determined minority. (Winham 1989: 64–65)

The actual course of negotiations of the UR between its launching in September 1986 and the approval of its Final Act in December 1993 was as tortuous; it was as full of conflicts and periodic breakdowns that threatened an end without agreement as the prenegotiation process that led to its launching. In accordance with the U.S.-India agreement, the Punta del Este declaration was in two sections: The first was launched by ministers and included services as a non-GATT subject of negotiations; the second was launched by the contracting parties to the GATT meeting at the ministerial level and included the rest of the negotiating agenda. The declaration repeated the principle of "differential and more favorable treatment" of developing countries as embodied in Part IV of the GATT and the "enabling clause" of the Tokyo Round agreement and also made reference to the special situation of the "least developed countries." Including services, there were fifteen negotiating mandates in the declaration; six related to market access, four to the reform of the GATT rules, three to the functioning of the GATT as an institution, and three to the "new issues" of trade-related intellectual property rights (TRIPs), trade-related investment measures (TRIMs), and services. Market-access mandates included agriculture, natural resources–based products, textiles and clothing, and tropical products, all of which were of interest to developing countries. The negotiations were to take place in Geneva with a midterm review in Montreal at a ministerial meeting in December 1988 and to be concluded in December 1990. In fact, by the time of the ministerial meeting in Brussels in December 1990, final agreements had been reached on almost none of the topics. The phase of negotiations from the Brussels meeting in December 1990 to the Geneva meeting in December 1993, at which the Final Act was agreed to, was not anticipated.

According to Low (1993: ch. 10), serious negotiations did not begin until 1988, and by December, when the ministers met in Montreal for the interim review, only six of the fifteen negotiating groups had clear texts for approval by the ministers. Also, the United States, by invoking the provisions of the Super 301 section of the Omnibus Trading Act of 1988 and naming Brazil, India, and Japan for possible retaliation for their alleged barriers to U.S. investment and inadequate protection to intellectual property rights, sent a powerful signal that it would aggressively pursue unilateral actions without necessarily first exhausting its options under the GATT or awaiting the outcome of negotiations on others. The meeting ended inconclusively with agreement in a few areas such as tropical products, interim reforms of the GATT dispute-settlement procedures, commitments to reduce tariffs on average by a third, and the provisional introduction of a new trade policy review mechanism (Schott 1994: 8). But agriculture, textiles, TRIPs, and safeguards, on which the ministers could not agree, were left to be pursued by Arthur Dunkel, the director-general of the GATT. He was instructed to report back to the Trade Negotiating Committee (TNC) in April 1989.

With an understanding between the United States and the EC on agriculture, Dunkel reported to the TNC that a basis existed for continuing negotiations on those issues. But this understanding soon evaporated, and attempts at new compromises failed. The TNC presented a 320-page document to the ministerial meeting in Brussels in December 1990, purportedly a draft of the Final Act of the UR negotiations but in fact containing little that could be called final (Low 1993: 229). Although progress was made at the meeting with respect to TRIPs, TRIMs, and services, the lack of agreement between the United States and the EC on agriculture led to a failure to conclude the round at the meeting. However, Dunkel was authorized to continue the search for solutions to outstanding issues and reconvene the TNC at his discretion.

Dunkel reconvened the TNC in April 1991 and restructured the negotiating groups to reduce them from fifteen to seven. With progress toward reforming its common agriculture policy, the EC and the United States made high-level efforts to resolve the agriculture deadlock. The G-7 summit of July 9, 1991, also emphasized the need for completing the UR. All these positive developments led Dunkel to set a December 1991 deadline for completion. This deadline also was not met; Dunkel issued a draft of the Final Act, its second version, but it too was incomplete. Besides not being a consensus document, it reflected Dunkel's compromise of the positions of the parties on various issues. As such it drew opposition from different parties to its different parts. At the TNC meeting in January 1992 it was evident that there was no agreement.

An accord between the United States and the EC on agriculture was reached in November 1992. But there was no progress on other issues in that year. The U.S. president's negotiating authority under the so-called fast-track procedure approved by the Congress was to expire on June 1, 1993. During spring 1993 the president asked Congress for an extension until December 15, 1993, which the Congress approved. The president also attended the Seattle summit of the Asia-Pacific Economic Cooperation (APEC) forum in November 1993, at which the Eminent Persons Group (appointed at the summit a year earlier) presented a report. The report recommended that APEC set a goal of free trade in the Asian Pacific, break the UR deadlock by offering an additional package of liberalization beyond UR proposals, and pursue an active program of regional trade liberalization. The success of the Seattle summit signaled to the EC that the United States and its APEC partners (accounting for 40 percent of world exports) had other options if the UR failed. This, the approaching date of expiration of fast-track negotiating authority, and the appointment of a very active new director-general of the GATT, namely Peter Sutherland, led to intensive negotiations in the second half of 1993 and culminated in the Final Act being agreed to in December 1993. The Cairns group (a coalition of agricultural exporters), founded in 1986 and consisting of Argentina, Australia, Brazil, Canada, Chile, Colombia, Fiji, Hungary, Indonesia, Malaysia, New Zealand, the Philippines, Thailand, and Uruguay, also helped in the successful conclusion of the UR by not letting the U.S.-EC farm disputes prevent an agreement on agriculture. It has also been suggested that the World Bank played a role in rounding up support for the Final Act from less developed countries.

The negotiating history of the UR illustrates the dynamics of the interests and concerns of individual countries (and groups tied together in regional trade agreements such as the EU) involved as well as the successful pursuit of Jackson's power-oriented approach by the major trading powers. As an example of the latter, almost all the eight rounds of the MTNs were the outcomes of U.S. initiatives and insistence. Also, in all earlier rounds of the MTNs, particularly the Tokyo Round,

> power came to be exercised in the negotiation through a pyramid structure whereby issues tended to be first negotiated between the U.S. and the EC; and once a tentative trade-off was established the negotiation process was progressively expanded to include other countries. In this way cooperation between the U.S. and the EC served to direct the negotiation. Where cooperation was not forthcoming between these economic "superpowers" the negotiation went nowhere because they had effective veto power; and when the two did agree, only the combined efforts of other parties (usually the developing countries) had any real prospect of setting the outcome. (Winham 1989: 54)

Of course, as was described earlier, the developing countries did not combine their efforts; they were split into the GT and the GF, the latter of which had twenty of their number. Their insistence on special and differential treatment and their reluctance to participate also did not help. The following description by one official of the prenegotiation period, as quoted by Winham (1989: 54), applied to the UR negotiation as well: "It was a brutal but salutary demonstration that power would be served in that nations comprising 5 percent of world trade were not able to stop a negotiation sought by nations comprising 95 percent of world trade."

The fact that members of the EC had differing perspectives on issues, most notably with respect to agriculture, meant that an internal agreement among the EC members was essential for progress to be made at the UR. But this also meant that once an internal agreement was struck, it became very difficult for the EC to deviate from its terms in the UR for fear of the agreement getting unraveled. This fear led to intransigence by the EC at the UR. More generally and parenthetically, it should be noted that the potential intransigence of regional groupings in multilateral negotiations arising from their internal differences is an aspect of regionalism that is detrimental to the multilateral trading system.

I turn now to the evolving dynamics of participants' interests. As noted earlier, GT, led by Brazil and India, did not attract more adherents in the prenegotiation phase up to Punt del Este. Subsequently, the approach of Brazil to the issues being negotiated shifted, reflecting a change of heart about the virtues of inward-oriented development strategies in Brazil and other major countries of Latin America. Sebastian Edwards (1995) argues that soul-searching about development began in Latin America in the early 1980s. It was driven by the failure of heterodox stabilization programs in Argentina, Brazil, and Peru; a realization of the contrast between the failure, by and large, of Latin America with inward-oriented policies and the rapid growth of East Asia with outward-oriented policies; and a better appreciation of the Chilean experience with market orientation. The citadel of inward orientation, namely the UN Commission for Latin America (CEPAL), published a major study in 1988 on the comparative experience of East Asia and Latin America based on the results of a collaborative research project between CEPAL and the Institute for Developing Economies in Tokyo. This was a pivotal event, according to Edwards. Brazil adopted a series of liberalizing reforms in 1990. In mid-1991, India, the other major bastion of inward orientation in GT, began dismantling its barriers to trade and direct foreign investment. Other developing countries had begun their trade reforms and unilateral liberalization even earlier. For these reforms in developing countries to succeed, a liberal world trading order was essential, and their full participation in the UR was a means of ensuring it.

As the UR negotiation wore on, the attitudes of some major developing countries with respect to some of the new issues also changed with several "coming to recognize that they might be able to develop a comparative advantage in certain services" (Haggard 1995: 44). The developing countries realized that their full participation in the multilateral negotiations of the UR in general and dispute-settlement and safeguards issues in particular was the only way to check the growth of aggressive unilateralism and the antidumping and countervailing duties in trade policy. Kahler (1995: 33) makes the same point when he says that

> both industrialized and developing countries sought to restrain American use of these instruments and to guarantee access to the American market. Also, the U.S. found that its competitors could easily mimic its policies: trading partners turned to their own versions of these instruments in classic tit-for-tat fashion. One route for restraint was regional free trade agreements; another was negotiation under the GATT.

With the realization on all sides that too much was at stake for the UR to be allowed to fail, an agreement was eventually reached.

5 *Achievements and Failures of the Uruguay Round: Market Access for Goods*

A number of studies assessing the Uruguay Round are available; Schott (1994) provides a succinct statement. Hoekman (1995) provides a comprehensive summary of the disciplines incorporated in the multilateral trade agreements (GATT, GATS, TRIMs, and TRIPs) that are under the umbrella of the WTO and evaluates the adequacy of various WTO rules and obligations from the perspective of economic efficiency and private-sector development. He also explores what could be done by a government to go beyond the WTO in achieving these goals. Martin and Winters (1996) summarize and synthesize the assessments of the papers presented at the World Bank conference on the UR held in early 1995. I have elsewhere (Srinivasan 1996a) gone over the same ground from the perspective of Asian developing economies. I draw on those studies and the GATT Secretariat (1994b: 6–7) and will therefore be brief here. The achievements with respect to market access were as follows.

Manufactured Goods

First, with respect to manufactured goods other than textiles, developed countries agreed to reduce their tariffs by 40 percent to an average of 3.8 percent from the pre-UR level of 6.3 percent.

Second, the proportion of such goods entering developed countries from *all sources* subject to *no* MFN tariffs would more than double from 20 percent to 44 percent, and the proportion subject to tariffs exceeding 15 percent would fall from 7 percent to 5 percent. The proportion of imports from *developing countries* facing a tariff exceeding 15 percent would fall from 9 percent to 5 percent.

Third, the percentage of bound tariffs on such goods in industrialized countries would increase from 78 percent to 99 percent. The corresponding rise in developing countries would be much more dramatic, from 21 percent to 73 percent.

Since the average tariffs on imports of manufactured goods from all sources were already low, that is, 6.3 percent in developed countries, their reduction by 40 percent is not particularly impressive. Also, Martin and Winters (1996) quote an estimate by M. Abreu that the reduction of tariffs on imports of manufactures from *developing countries* was only 30 percent. They note that although there was some success for developing countries in terms of an absolute reduction in the degree of tariff escalation in the imports of manufactures into developed countries, a modest escalation still remains. With respect to bindings, once again, since developed countries had already bound most of their tariffs prior to the UR, there was not much room for an increase. Still, the dramatic increase in the proportion of bound tariffs in the case of developing countries is a significant achievement even if it is tempered by the fact the tariffs have been bound at fairly high levels.

Agriculture

Governments in developed and developing countries have massively intervened in agriculture. It is no surprise, therefore, that "agriculture has been virtually excluded from the broad sweep of trade liberalization and insulated from the normal disciplines of market forces and international competition" (GATT 1979: 7). As noted earlier, disagreements between the EU and the United States on liberalizing agriculture and bringing it under the GATT disciplines considerably delayed and almost wrecked the successful conclusion of the UR (for a history of agriculture in the GATT see Hathaway 1987).

The UR agreement on agriculture is claimed to "provide a framework for the long-term reform of agricultural trade and domestic policies over the years to come. It makes a decisive move towards the objective of increased market orientation in agricultural trade. The rules governing agricultural trade are strengthened which will lead to improved predictability and stability for importing and exporting countries alike" (GATT 1994c: 8). It encourages the use of fewer trade-distorting domestic support measures, although countries are allowed some flexibility, albeit under rather stringent conditions, in implementing the change.

The most important component of the agreement ostensibly is the requirement that all nontariff border measures be replaced by tariffs that initially provide the same level of protection. Tariffs resulting from this "tariffication" process and other agricultural tariffs are to be reduced for developed and developing countries over a period of six and ten years by an *average* of 36 percent and 24 percent, respectively, and minimum reductions are required under each tariff line. Although existing market-access opportunities are to be maintained under a "special treatment" clause, a country is allowed to retain import restrictions until the end of the implementation period under certain carefully and strictly defined circumstances. Developing countries are afforded special and differential treatment that in effect exempts them from the commitment to liberalize with respect to any agricultural product that is a predominant staple in their traditional diet.

Unfortunately, the loopholes in the process of tariffication have allowed countries to bind tariffs at levels much above the prevailing average in many cases. Two countries, Japan and Korea, have even succeeded in negotiating a delay in tariffication of their very high barriers to rice imports. A few egregious examples, drawn from Hathaway and Ingco (1996: Tables 2.2a and 2.2b, 43–44), of base ad valorem equivalent tariffs (BTs)—on which the Uruguay Round tariff reductions may be based—that were higher than the actual average (AA) prevailing in a given country during 1986–1988 are as follows: As against an AA of only 3 percent on beef and veal, the United States chose a BT of 31 percent. The European Union chose a BT of 361 percent on rice as compared to an AA of 153 percent. Developing countries were no better. Thailand, a rice *exporter*, chose to set a BT of 58 percent as against an AA of 3 percent on rice imports.

The UR agreement goes beyond border measures that are traditionally the targets of the GATT disciplines in bringing some restraint on domestic-support measures as well. Such measures with only a minimal or no impact on trade (the so-called green-box policies) need not be reduced. In particular, income support to agricultural producers that is "decoupled" from production could continue. Research, disease-control, infrastructure, and food-security policies are among the green-box policies. Other policies, such as direct payments to limit production and those that encourage agricultural and rural development, are also excluded from the purview of reduction commitments as long as they do not in all account for more than 5 and 10 percent, respectively, of the value of production in developed and developing countries. Developed and developing countries must reduce nonexcluded support by 20 and 13.3 percent, respectively, during the implementation period.

As in tariffication, there appear to be loopholes in the implementation of reductions in domestic-support measures. Main farm programs of the United States and the EU are exempted, and Japan has even increased its direct payments to farmers. Of course, the least-developed countries are not required to make any reduction. Whereas in the case of manufacturers, direct export subsidies are outlawed, subsidies for agricultural exports by developed and developing countries are merely to be reduced, respectively, over six and ten years to a level 36 and 24 percent below the 1986–1990 base period level; the quantity of subsidized exports is to be reduced by 21 and 14 percent, respectively. However, it would appear that these commitments are likely to be the most liberalizing, since they are much harder to evade. Once again, least-developed countries are exempted.

Integrating agricultural trade with the WTO, thereby bringing some discipline to government interventions, is a major achievement. The formally agreed-upon extent of liberalization does appear substantial. Yet with high levels of bound or base-level tariffs resulting from the loophole-ridden tariffication process, fairly long implementation periods, permitted exemptions, and the exclusion of some trade-distorting policies from elimination, it is hard to escape the conclusion that the extent of liberalization is likely to be insignificant. The fact that permitted exemptions and exclusions can be applied only under special and narrowly defined circumstances is likely to moderate, but not eliminate, their use.

Indeed, model-based simulations of the long-term effects from liberalization show virtually no gains. Most of these simulations consider only the liberalization of direct interventions in agricultural trade. However, as Anne Krueger and her colleagues (1988) have shown, the protection or disprotection of agriculture in developing countries arising from indirect measures (such as exchange-rate overvaluation and protection of industry) was much stronger than that arising from direct measures. Fortunately, the liberalization of nonagricultural trade envisaged under the Final Act will reduce the indirect distortion of agricultural trade to some extent.

There have been many studies estimating the effects of liberalizing agricultural trade. Some (Parikh et al. 1988 and those reported in Goldin and Knudsen 1990) were done prior to the completion of the Uruguay Round. Others (e.g., Brandão and Martin 1993) were based on the extent of liberalization in the draft of the Uruguay Round agreement (proposed by Arthur Dunkel, at the time the director-general of the GATT) rather than the actual offers and commitments in the Final Act as signed.

Table 5.1 presents the broad orders of magnitude of the impact of the liberalization as assessed by the most recent studies. These studies translate the various components of the schedules of bindings, offers, and commitments into reductions in trade barriers as specified in their models.[1] These studies include Brown and others (1996); François, McDonald, and Nordström (1996); Goldin and Mensbrugghe (1996); and Harrison, Rutherford, and Tarr (1996). Their models differ in many respects: levels of aggregation with respect to consumers, commodities, and countries; parameter estimates, including in particular their actual or implied elasticities of supply, demand, or substitution in production or consumption; assumptions regarding scale economies and market structure; their base periods; and others. Although the absolute magnitudes of the changes in production, consumption, trade, and welfare are noncomparable across

TABLE 5.1   Welfare (Real Income) Effects of Liberalization of Agricultural Trade

Country/Region	Brown et al. (1996) ($ billion)[a]	François et al. (1996) (% of GDP)[b]	Goldin and Mensbrugghe (1996) (% of GDP)[c]	Harrison et al. (1996) ($ billion)[d]
Developed countries				
Australia and				
New Zealand	−0.197	(0.18, 0.27)	(0.0, 0.6)	(1.015, 1.343)
Canada	−0.514	(0.07, 0.13)	(−0.2, 0.4)	(0.211, 0.238)
European Union	−0.899	(0.01, 0.11)	(0.1, 1.9)	(26.753, 28.530)
Japan	12.290	(−0.02, −0.01)	(0.2, 1.6)	(15.232, 16.897)
USA		(−0.01, −0.00)	(0.0, 0.2)	(1.659, 3.031)
Asian developing countries				
China			(−0.1, −0.2)	(−0.561, −0.835)
India			(0.0, 0.8)	
Indonesia			(0.1, 0.5)	(0.170, 0.299)
Korea				(4.604, 5.222)
Malaysia				(1.225, 2.199)
Philippines				(0.618, 1.065)
Taiwan				(0.011, 0.012)
Thailand				(0.047, 1.284)
Asian NICs	0.199			
East Asia		(0.00, 0.06)		
South Asia		(−0.10, −0.05)		(−0.134, 0.097)
Low-income Asia			(0.0, 0.4)	
Upper-income Asia			(0.8, 4.9)	
Other regions				
Sub-Saharan Africa				(−0.637, −0.292)
Africa		(−0.10, 0.23)	(−0.5, −0.2)	
Latin America		(0.02, 0.19)	(−0.3, 0.4)	
World		(0.02, 0.04)		(58.309, 62.74)

[a]The European Union figure includes Norway and Switzerland. Asian newly industrializing countries include Hong Kong, South Korea, Singapore, and Taiwan.

[b]The interval covers the range of estimated welfare effects in six variants, three each for constant returns to scale and perfect competition and for increasing returns to scale and imperfect-competition models. Within each model the variants cover the case of no change in capital stock, two cases of endogenous changes in capital stock, one brought about by fixed savings rates, and the other by endogenously changing savings rates.

[c]The interval covers the range of estimates from six scenarios that vary in the base-level tariffs from which the Uruguay Round reductions take place, whether or not inputs subsidies are included, and so on. Africa in this column excludes Nigeria and South Africa, and Latin America excludes Brazil and Mexico.

[d]The interval covers the two estimates from the base model and the steady-state version of the base model. Except for the European Union, steady effects were always larger.

studies, the changes relative to some normalizing magnitudes, such as GDP, and magnitudes in a base scenario of no change in policies are likely to be comparable. The results reported in Table 5.1 are to be assessed with these caveats in mind.

The striking feature of Table 5.1 is the relatively small effect of liberalization, reflecting the fact that once "dirty tariffication" and exemptions are taken into account, the extent of liberalization is modest. Although there are some changes of sign across models of the effects on particular countries or regions, almost all the estimates for Africa are negative, though not large.

Textiles and Clothing

This is perhaps the most important sector from the perspective of developing economies in general and poorer Asian developing economies (ADEs) in particular. The percentage share of merchandise exports accounted for by textiles and clothing for the ADEs was as follows in 1993 or thereabouts (World Bank 1994; World Bank 1995: Table 15): Bangladesh, 78; Hong Kong, 40; India, 30; Indonesia, 17; Republic of Korea, 19; Malaysia, 6; Nepal, 84; Pakistan, 78; Philippines, 10; Singapore, 5; and Sri Lanka, 52. As is by now well known, what started out as a short-term agreement in 1961 mainly to restrain the growth of Japanese exports of cotton textiles soon became a long-term agreement and by 1974 had expanded to include trade in textiles and clothing made with other fibers (natural and synthetic). Thus this short-term agreement became the Multifibre Arrangement (MFA), under which each exporting country gets *and* administers a *bilaterally* agreed-upon quota of exports to each market. Over time the MFA became increasingly restrictive. MFA IV expired at the end of 1994.

The UR agreement envisages the phaseout of MFA in three stages over a period of ten years from January 1, 1995. During each stage, annual *growth rate* in the import quotas on those products that are still under restraint will be increased by no less than 16 percent per year over MFA IV in Stage 1 (until 1988), by no less than 25 percent over Stage 1 in Stage 2 (January 1, 1998–December 31, 2001), and by no less than 27 percent over Stage 2 in Stage 3 (January 1, 2002–December 31, 2004). As soon as the agreement comes into force, products that accounted for not less than 16 percent of 1990 imports will be integrated into the GATT. At the beginning of Stage 2, a further 17 percent will be integrated, and at the beginning of Stage 3, another 18 percent. All the remaining products will be integrated on January 1, 2005. At each of the first three stages, products are to be chosen from each of the following categories: tops and yarns, fabrics, made-up textile products, and clothing.

The phaseout of MFA is backloaded (in fact, products accounting for as much as 49 percent of the value of 1990 imports could still be under quota restrictions as of the end of the ten-year period, i.e., on December 31, 2004!); the accelerated growth in quotas during the transition period will not only yield substantial benefits but could also make lobbying harder for the interest groups opposed to the abolition of MFA. They may have to lobby for an extension of the quota system of MFA *and* for a slowdown in the growth of quotas, a difficult task.[2] The transitional "safeguard" mechanism, part of the agreement, could be invoked (albeit under restrictive conditions) to slow down the phaseout even further. However, quotas imposed under these safeguards have to be terminated by January 1, 2005. Thus they cannot be used to extend the MFA. Antidumping measures can be invoked, however, as they already have been by the EC with respect to gray cotton fabric (Hindley 1997a, 1997b). Although substantial opportunities for increasing textile and clothing exports for poorer ADEs, particularly from South Asia, are likely to arise in the coming decade, the political economy of textile protectionism in industrialized countries suggests caution; with a decade to go before the scheduled date of the abolition of MFA, forces opposed to it may indeed gather enough strength to prevent it. I come back to this issue in Chapter 12.

A number of studies on the restrictive effects of the MFA on exporters and on the welfare of consumers in individual countries and the likely consequences of the MFA's phaseout are available (Cline 1990; De Melo and Tarr 1990; François, McDonald, and Nordström 1996; Goto 1989; Harrison, Rutherford, and Tarr 1996; Hertel et al. 1996; Hufbauer and Elliott 1994; Trela and Whalley 1990; and Whalley 1995). The most recent of these estimates are shown in Table 5.2. As is to be expected, the estimates from different models differ both in magnitude and sometimes in sign. Yet they agree in projecting a substantial gain for the United States and the European Union. Sub-Saharan Africa and Latin America stand to lose.

Srinivasan and Canonero (1995) project a substantial increase in trade in textiles and clothing for the South Asian economies once such trade is liberalized. Their projections are based on their parameter estimates from a gravity model of bilateral-trade flows during 1968–1991. The expected increases in clothing exports as a percentage of total bilateral trade of selected South Asian countries consequent to liberalization by their major partners in the industrial world can be seen in Table 5.3.

Although these figures are impressive, caution is needed in interpreting them, since the existing quotas under MFA permit exports also from countries that are not internationally competitive. With its phaseout, a very competitive export market will emerge. Unless poorer Asian exporters can compete in cost as well as quality, they might not be able to maintain, let alone increase, their share in growing world export markets.

TABLE 5.2 Welfare Effects of Liberalization of Trade in Textiles and Apparel

Country/Region	*François et al. (1996) (% of GDP)[a]*	*Harrison et al. (1996) ($ billion)[b]*	*Hertel et al. (1996) (% of GDP)*
Developed countries			
European Union	(0.09, 0.28)	(7.624, 7.880)	0.32
Japan	(−0.02, 0.12)	(−0.531, −0.517)	0.03
USA	(0.12, 0.38)	(9.469, 10.136)	
			0.29
Canada	(−0.03, 0.17)	(0.939, 1.031)	
Asian developing countries			
China	(0.74, 4.28)	(0.876, 1.578)	0.42
East Asia	(−0.01, 3.34)		
Hong Kong		(−1.698, −1.463)	
Indonesia		(0.617, 0.897)	1.10
Malaysia		(0.082, 0.226)	−0.63
Philippines		(−0.002, 0.233)	−0.18
Singapore		(−0.151, −0.149)	
South Asia	(0.44, 4.10)	(0.629, 1.473)	0.35
Taiwan		(−0.450, −0.285)	
Thailand		(0.065, 0.824)	0.32
Other regions			
Latin America	(−0.02, 0.14)	(−0.498, −0.411)	−0.27
Sub-Saharan Africa		(−0.231, −0.112)	−0.24
Africa	(−0.01, 0.28)		
World	(0.08, 0.52)	(15.950, 19.626)	0.59

[a]The interval covers the range of estimated welfare effects in six variants, three each for constant returns to scale and perfect competition and for increasing returns to scale and imperfect-competition models. Within each model the variants cover the case of no change in capital stock, two cases of endogenous changes in capital stock, one brought about by fixed savings rates, and the other by endogenously changing savings rates.

[b]The interval covers the range of estimates from six scenarios that vary in the base-level tariffs from which the Uruguay Round reductions take place, whether or not inputs subsidies are included and so on.

TABLE 5.3 Projected Increases in Trading in Clothing for Selected South Asian Economies After MFA Liberalization (percentages of total bilateral trade)

Trading Partners	Bangladesh	India	Nepal	Pakistan	Sri Lanka
USA	12.9	2.6	8.4	3.5	9.0
EC	9.8	4.3	10.0	6.4	3.8
Japan	0.1	0.1	0.1	0.1	0.1

SOURCE: Srinivasan and Canonero (1995).

Overall Real Income Effects of UR Trade Liberalization

Early estimates of the overall gains in real income and growth in world trade volume expected from the UR trade liberalization were provided by the GATT secretariat (*GATT* 1994b: 6). These estimates suggest the following:

- The increase in world income from the liberalization of trade in goods will range from a low of $109 billion to a high of $510 billion in 2005 (the end of the implementation period), depending on the economic model used. The GATT secretariat views the assumptions underlying the upper end of the range as more realistic.
- Associated with the upper end of the range of estimated annual income gains is a gain of $122 billion for the United States, $164 billion for the European communities, $27 billion for Japan, and $116 billion for developing and transition economies as a group.
- The estimated increase in the volume of world trade in goods, once the liberalization has been fully implemented, ranges from 9 to 24 percent; in terms of *actual 1992* trade flows, the gains would range from $244 billion to $668 billion. Since trade in 2005 will be greater than trade in 1992 in any case, if we start from the larger base, the increases due to the liberalization effected by the UR are very likely to be larger.
- All versions of the model estimate the percentage increase in the exports and imports of the developing and transition economies as a group to be 50 percent above the average increase for the world as a whole.

The same document suggests that even the high estimate of a $510 billion increase in global income is an understatement of the likely actual gains from the UR for three reasons. First, the estimate ignores dynamic effects. Second, the avoidance of a large loss that would have been the inevitable consequence of the failure of the round should be counted as part of the gains from the round. Third, the gains arising from other aspects of the Final Act besides liberalization of trade in goods are ignored.

Other model-based simulations of the short-term and long-term effects are provided in Tables 5.4 and 5.5. The striking, though not particularly surprising, feature of the simulation exercises in these tables is the extremely modest (as a proportion of GDP) gains from trade liberalization, particularly in models that assume constant returns to scale in production and perfect competition in all markets.

Many previous simulations of the effects of trade liberalization, regional integration, and tax reforms for individual countries as well as regions, go-

TABLE 5.4   Estimates of the Annual Benefits of Uruguay Round
Trade Liberalization

		Increase in Real Income[a]		
Model/Variant	*Year*	*World*	*Industrial*	*Developing*[b]
WTO (François et al. 1996)				
Static, perfect competition	1992	40	27	13
		(0.17)	(0.16)	(0.30)
Static, imperfect competition	1992	99	40	59
		(0.44)	(0.23)	(1.23)
Induced investment,	1992	214	90	125
imperfect condition		(0.94)	(0.5)	(2.6)
Bank (Harrison et al. 1996)				
Static, perfect competition	1992	93	75	18
		(0.40)	(0.41)	(0.38)
Static, imperfect competition	1992	96	77	19
		(0.42)	(0.42)	(0.42)
Induced investment,	1992	171	115	55
imperfect condition		(0.74)	(0.61)	(1.20)
GTAP (Hertel et al. 1996)				
Liberalization in projection	2005	258	172	86
to 2005, perfect competition		(0.89)	(0.72)	(1.56)

[a]Billions of U.S. dollars at 1992 prices (percentages of GDP in parentheses).
[b]Definitions of developing countries differ slightly between models.
SOURCE: Martin and Winters (1996), Table 1.1. Reprinted by permission.

ing way back to the estimates of Harry Johnson (1958) of the effect on the
United Kingdom of freer trade with Europe, also showed very modest effects. However, since the gains that do occur are pure efficiency gains, even
a gain of, for example, 0.7 percent of GDP, as in Table 5.5 for the world,
compares favorably with the as yet unachieved and unlikely to ever be
achieved target for external assistance of 0.7 percent of GDP for developed
countries! Be that as it may, there are a number of reasons the actual gains
might be substantially higher than those estimated from the models, including, importantly, the gains from the release for productive use of resources that would continue to be engaged in rent-seeking were there to be
no liberalization. It is also seen from Table 5.4 that, not surprisingly, allowing for investment to respond to the opportunities created by liberalization
and departing from the assumption of perfect competition increase the estimated gains. However, the parametric and other assumptions involved in
incorporating investment and imperfect competition are often stronger and
based on less firm empirical foundations than those on which static, per-
fect-competition models are based. Other than as indicating orders of magnitude of the gains around which there is likely to be a wide band of error,
these estimates have to be used with extreme caution in policy discussions.

TABLE 5.5 Real Income Gains from Uruguay Round Trade Liberalization by Region

Country/Region	Welfare Gains ($mil 1992)	Welfare Gains (% of GDP)
Australia	3.3	1.0
New Zealand	1.4	3.5
Canada	2.6	0.4
USA	26.7	0.4
Japan	22.7	0.6
Republic of Korea	7.5	2.4
European Union	49.9	0.7
Indonesia	2.6	2.0
Malaysia	5.0	8.8
Philippines	2.4	4.2
Singapore	0.7	1.7
Thailand	12.6	10.7
China	2.0	0.4
Hong Kong	−1.1	−1.2
Taiwan	1.1	0.5
Argentina	2.3	1.0
Brazil	4.3	1.0
Mexico	2.3	0.6
Rest of Latin America	4.7	1.6
Sub-Saharan Africa	−0.7	−0.5
Middle East and North Africa	1.5	0.2
Eastern Europe and former Soviet Union	1.2	0.1
South Asia	6.7	1.8
Other European	8.8	0.7
Developing countries (total)	55.2	1.1
Industrialized countries (total)	115.4	0.6
World	170.6	0.7

SOURCE: Harrison, Rutherford, and Tarr (1996), Table 8.7. Reprinted by permission.

Notes

1. I will not discuss the models, since even to describe each model meaningfully, let alone their differences and their relative strengths and weaknesses, would require a lot of space! Their weaknesses notwithstanding, there is no alternative to an economy-wide and global modeling exercise for assessing the *overall effect of simultaneous change in many trade policies of several countries.*

2. I thank Will Martin for drawing my attention to these aspects of quota growth.

6 Issues Other than Market Access for Goods: Services, TRIMs and TRIPs, Safeguards, Dispute-Settlement, and Nontariff Measures

Services

Trade in services (defined as nonfactor services in the balance of payments minus government transactions) grew at an annual average rate of 8.3 percent between 1980 and 1992, a faster growth rate than that of merchandise trade (Hoekman 1996). Although the share of developing countries in service trade declined during the same period, it is still over 10 percent. The objective of the General Agreement on Trade in Services (GATS) is to establish a multilateral framework that is analogous to that for trade in goods. However, evaluating the extent of liberalization of trade in services envisaged in the agreement, offers and commitments received thus far, and their effects is difficult in comparison with trade in goods. The reason is that there is no equivalent of a tariff as a barrier to market access in services. The significant barriers arise from the bewildering variety of applicable domestic laws and regulations. Further, the available data on trade in services are incomplete, unreliable, and noncomparable across countries and over time. Data are available only on service transactions between entities that are located in different countries. Except for the United States, no data are available on the local sales of foreign affiliates. A comprehensive discussion of many of the conceptual and practical issues involved in liberalizing service trade is available in UNCTAD (1993). According to this document, Asian developing economies (ADEs) accounted for 7.1 percent of world trade in commercial services in 1990,

7.3 percent in shipment, 6.7 percent in passenger and other transport, 7.9 percent in travel, 6.2 percent in labor and property income, and 3.0 percent in other services. The share of merchandise exports of the ADEs was 7.5 percent in 1990. Thus service trade recorded in the balance-of-payments data is quite important for the ADEs. Of the forty leading exporters of commercial services in the world, nine were Asian.

Hoekman (1996) provides an in-depth assessment of the GATS. According to him, the GATS applies to measures that affect the consumption of services in a member country that originate in other member countries. It covers all modes of supply, namely cross-border supply without the physical movement of consumer or supplier, supply involving the movement of the consumer to the country of the supplier, services sold in one member country by legal entities with a commercial presence in that country but originating in another member country, and services requiring the temporary migration of "natural" persons. The agreement consists of a set of *general* concepts, principles, and rules of applicability across the board; *specific* commitments on national treatment (NT) and market access applicable to those sectors or subsectors listed in a member's schedule subject to any qualifications or conditions; an *understanding* of possible future negotiations to liberalize service trade further; and a set of attachments including annexes listing specific sectoral commitments and ministerial decisions relating to the implementation of the GATS.

It is clear that although the core principles of the GATT, namely MFN and NT, apply generally in the GATS, they are heavily qualified. First, within sixty days beginning four months after entry into force of the UR agreement, each member can exempt any *service* from the application of the MFN, and further exemptions can be sought through the normal waiver procedure. Second, within the same period, a member can improve, modify, or withdraw all or part of its specific commitments on financial services.

At the end of UR, seventy-six countries offered commitments on financial services. The United States viewed the commitments of some members to be insufficiently forthcoming to warrant a final settlement. The United States had announced in 1993 that it would not extend its commitments on an MFN basis unless the offers of other countries were improved. This in effect meant that the United States would discriminate among foreign financial service providers. To avoid this outcome, the deadline for entering MFN exemptions and amending commitments was extended to June 1995. Even the improvements made by that date in the commitments of other members did not prove satisfactory to the United States, and it announced that it would withdraw most of its offers on financial services and take an MFN exemption for the whole financial sector. Because of the possibility that others might follow the United States and downgrade their commitments, the EC proposed an extension of the deadline by a month to see whether the agreement could be salvaged with or without the participation of the United States. With the United States still not satisfied, but for other industrialized countries, including Japan, sticking to their commitments, the financial services agreement would have collapsed. The agreement is due to expire in December 1997.

Third, NT applies to only those sectors and subsectors listed in a member's schedule, and even then only insofar as existing measures are not exempted. With diversity among members in their GDP levels, the share of tradable services in their GDP, and their sectoral and subsectoral commitments, exemptions, and so on, it is not a simple matter to calculate the extent of coverage of the MFN and NT commitments across country groups. At one extreme, if one were to use the magnitude of commitments where no restrictions apply to both market access and national treatment as a measure of how close the GATS will take its members to free trade, Hoekman's (1996) estimates are not very encouraging. Eighteen high-income countries (HICs)—including the Organization for Economic Cooperation and Development (with the EC counted as one), Singapore, Hong Kong, and Korea—placed *no* restrictions on market access, only on 30.5 percent of the total number of services in the list established by the Group of Negotiations on Services (GNS). The corresponding figure for all other countries (including most developing countries) was far less, that is, 6.7 percent. With respect to national treatment, the figures were not much higher; the HIC percentage was 35.3 and that of all other countries, 8.5. Hoekman's calculations of sectoral commitments adjusted for mode of supply, the proportion of service sectors exempted from liberalization, and the sector's weight in GDP resulted in the following percentage of commitments relative to the total number in the GNS list.

	HICs	Developing Countries
Market Access	48.5	11.4
National Treatment	53.0	12.6

Although these figures are far lower than the corresponding ones for goods trade, still they are sizable compared with a situation of no commitment, which would have prevailed had there been no agreement.

Brown and colleagues (1996) estimate that real income gains from *future* liberalization (and not just from what was agreed to in the UR) in services will be $39 billion for Europe, $37 billion for the United States, $22 billion for Japan, $9 billion for Canada, $5 billion for Australia and New Zealand, and $24 billion for the rest of the world. Together these gains amount to a global total of $136 billion, which is more than half their estimate of the gain from liberalization of all trade including agriculture, manufactures, and services.

Hoekman (1996) notes that market-access commitments by OECD countries tend to be more restrictive with respect to services in which developing countries have an actual or potential comparative advantage, such as services that are intensive in labor (skilled and unskilled) but that require a temporary permit for workers to be able to sell their services in importing countries. But Hoekman is certainly right in his assertion that most of the immediate potential gains for developing countries would arise in further liberalization of access to their own service markets. He is also right in drawing attention to other disquieting, though easily addressed, features of the GATS, particularly its allowing members not to bind the status quo in many sectors. It is to be hoped that members will muster enough political courage to push forward toward free trade in services in their future negotiations.

Schott's (1994: 111) assessment is similar to Hoekman's. He concludes that the GATS achieved mixed results with regard to improved rules and market access commitments in particular service sectors. The scope of specific market-access commitments varies by sector from extensive (e.g., in professional services) to minimal (e.g., in audiovisual services). Results in other important sectors such as financial services and maritime services are incomplete and show little promise for fuller gains in the negotiations scheduled to end in 1995 and 1996, respectively. The GATS implicitly allows for cross-retaliation between goods and service sectors. The cross-retaliation provision can be invoked only if a member does not abide by a panel finding. Besides, it is conditional; it can be used only if it is not possible to retaliate within the covered sector. Still, it could be used against developing countries (e.g., for their violation of the GATS, their goods trade could be penalized).

A somewhat more optimistic, though still cautious, view of the GATS is that of Low (1995: 49), who points out that

> commitments under GATS have created a benchmark [that] guarantees defined levels of market access, and against which future liberalization can be undertaken. The use of a positive list for specific commitments offers less transparency than would a negative list, but this is partly mitigated by the negative list approach to the scheduling of market access and national treatment limitations. The "double exit" possibilities offered by selective scheduling (combined with relatively few rules for general application) together with market access and national treatment limitations in schedules will become less permissive as sectoral coverage expands. But there is also scope for enhancing liberalization through the imposition of more stringent rules on the nature of limitations on market access and national treatment, especially if the role of price-based over quantity-based limitations were to be emphasized.

Trade-Related Investment Measures (TRIMs)
and Trade-Related Intellectual Property Rights (TRIPs)

Evaluating TRIMs and TRIPs involves difficulties similar to those applicable to services. Both were "new" issues that at the time of the Punta del Este declaration were seen as requiring the discipline of the multilateral framework. The UR agreement affects domestic rules and regulations in those areas and formally extends the core principles of the GATT. But this extension is neither complete nor absolute. Braga (1996) argues that implementation of TRIPs not only would require significant reforms of the intellectual property regimes of developing countries but from a static perspective would also result in rent transfer from developing to developed countries, although the relatively long period of implementation allowed for developing countries will attenuate this loss. However, the dynamic gain from TRIPs could be significant if, as the recent models of growth and development emphasize, the driving force of sustained growth is accumulation of "knowledge capital" through domestic research, import, and imitation (when appropriate).

In models with spillover effects, knowledge created anywhere has potentially beneficial effects everywhere. To the extent that subscribing to TRIPs (and to TRIMs, since foreign direct investment is also a means of technology transfer) makes the accumulation of knowledge capital more rapid, it will be beneficial to all developing countries. Many of the ADEs with their relatively better endowment of skills and knowledge capital as compared with the rest of the developing world are likely to reap a significant share of the benefits. Also, adhering to the provisions of the agreement on TRIMs and TRIPs will make investment in the ADEs more attractive to foreigners. Whether the likely short-run adverse effects in terms of price rises in sectors such as pharmaceuticals are quantitatively significant is not easy to discern.

Subramanian (1995: 39–40) argues that although the negotiations were riven in conflict, they

> produced a comprehensive agreement [on intellectual property] with very high standards of protection, providing for the first time detailed rules for national enforcement procedures . . . [given] one choice . . . between addressing it multilaterally in the Uruguay Round or bilaterally with major trading partners. . . . Developing countries preferred the multilateral approach. . . . With agreement . . . on TRIPS . . . there will be greater disciplines on the use of unilateral actions in the area of Intellectual Property. . . . In return for making concessions on TRIPS, developing countries gained in areas of export interest to them—textiles, clothing and agriculture—a general perception remains that a strong regime of property rights is essential [for] attracting foreign investment and foreign technology. . . . TRIPS [agreement

offers] developing countries opportunities where they would gain as exporters of IP-related products.

Low and Subramanian (1996) and Low (1995) find that the TRIMs negotiations produced an outcome that was more modest than was hoped for at Punta del Este and largely reaffirmed certain preexisting disciplines. Nonetheless, establishing some international rules such as TRIMs strengthens the opportunities for members to benefit from international specialization, as the GATT did for trade in goods. However, whether the rules should be extended to domestic competition policy, and in particular whether such policies should be harmonized, are debatable issues. Since many of the restrictions that developing (and some developed) countries place on foreign investors (such as local content requirements) rarely make sense, even in a "second-best" environment, their elimination under TRIMs should be beneficial. Low and Subramanian rightly characterize the failure of TRIMs to address export performance requirements as the most serious. It is to be hoped, once again, as in the case of GATS, that future negotiations will expand TRIMs and TRIPs in the direction of further liberalization.

Safeguards

If one were asked to cite three fundamental principles of the GATT, one would almost surely list nondiscrimination enshrined in the principle of MFN (Article I, paragraph 1), NT on internal taxation and regulation (Article III, paragraph 4), and the prohibition of all border measures other than duties, taxes, or other charges on external trade (Article XI, paragraph 1). Besides these principles, transparency of border measures is mandated (Article X). Yet as Abbott (1995) rightly emphasizes, the GATT also authorizes a variety of measures that are at odds with these lofty principles. Article XXIV, on permitting customs unions and free trade areas, violates MFN. Quantitative restrictions (QRs) such as import and export quotas ruled out under Article XI are allowed under the balance-of-payments provisions of Articles XII and XVIII. The general exceptions under Article XX and national security exceptions under Article XXI are other provisions that authorize departures from the fundamental principles. Article XIX was intended as a 'safeguard to enable temporary exceptions when a surge in imports threatens serious injury to contracting parties. Article XXVIII allows a party to withdraw or modify concessions it made earlier. Finally, Article XXXV allows a member a one-time-only freedom not to apply concessions it offered at the time of its own accession to another party that accedes later; this freedom can be exercised only at the time that the nonmember becomes a member. Article VI allows a contracting party to levy an antidumping duty on a product that is "dumped" or a countervailing duty on a product that is subsidized by another party when such dumping or subsidizing causes or threatens material injury to an established domestic industry.

Interestingly, even though it is relatively easy to invoke Article XIX on safeguard measures (SGMs)—all that is necessary is to establish serious injury to domestic industry by a surge in imports with no need to relate the surge to foreign "unfair" practices such as dumping or subsidizing— it has been invoked very rarely. Instead, the so-called gray-area measures ("gray" because they are not prima facie inconsistent with the letter of the GATT) such as "voluntary" export restraints (VERs) and "voluntary" import expansions (VIEs), as well as GATT-consistent antidumping measures, or ADMs (under Article VI), have been frequently used, particularly by industrialized countries. Abbott (1995: 2) goes on to say that

> in effect, ADM's have become the trade remedy of choice for import-competing firms and their governments in the West. Developing nations, especially in Asia, have been frequent targets of ADM, and rightly see them as a significant threat to liberalization. At the same time, however, a number of developing countries—in Asia—as well as in Latin America and other regions are moving rapidly to adopt and implement this form of market intervention, raising increasing concern within the industrialized West.

The safeguards agreement (SGA) of the UR is clearly intended to bring SGMs firmly within the ambit of Article XIX by prohibiting VERs, VIEs, and other gray-area measures. It balances this prohibition by easing at the same time some of the political constraints on the imposition of safeguard measures. While restraining flagrant abuses of ADMs, it liberalizes the terms and allows greater flexibility of their use by national authorities. Abbott (1995) points to the authorities in the United States and to a lesser extent in the European Union as having taken advantage of the UR provisions on ADMs to maintain and even add restrictive elements in their antidumping laws. He finds that "as a result, the 'bottom-line,' i.e. the net effects of the UR agreement, is far from clear."

Abbott (1995: 3) concludes that

> the continued use of expansive ADM in the West, and the growing use of ADM by developing countries in Asia and other parts of the world, pose significant risks to the multilateral trading system—threatening its goals of liberalization, transparency and non-discrimination—even as that system moves into an historic new phase of liberalization. . . . ADM in the West should be constrained and if possible rolled back; and . . . developing countries should be dissuaded from following in the steps of their Western trading partners, or at least similarly constrained in their use of ADM. It is almost a corollary of this position that SGM, especially as regulated in the

SGA, are a superior means of coping with the social, political and economic strains of liberalization.

Trade remedy laws in Asia are still in flux; it may yet be possible to prevent the adoption and implementation of anti-dumping laws in ways that will undercut the region's growing liberalization. The primary strategy in this effort must be to persuade influential audiences in Asia to slow their nations' rush to ADM.

Finger (1996) comes to a similar conclusion. In his comprehensive discussion of all safeguard provisions, he notes that the efforts during the Uruguay Round negotiation to restrict the use of antidumping measures met with little success. The Final Act certainly sets public-notice and transparency requirements and a five-year sunset clause on antidumping (AD) actions. But Finger suggests that these are not as far reaching as they may seem. First, as long as GATT panels continue to treat procedural errors in AD actions as merely calling for rectification of errors or recalculation of AD duties, rather than removing them, stricter procedural requirements such as transparency and public notice are unlikely to deter a protectionist use of AD. And the sunset clause has little bite, since there is virtually no limit to the number of times an AD measure can be reviewed and extended.

AD enforcement is based on *national* AD laws and so is likely to favor concentrated producer interests rather than diffused consumer interests. Thus, as Finger argues, producers will treat protection through AD action as their *entitlement* and make it politically costly for the executive and legislative branches to liberalize or repeal AD laws. In fact, they will lobby at home for national AD laws that make it easier to prove dumping and initiate AD action. During the negotiations of the Uruguay Round, the same lobbyists were also active abroad in Geneva, seeking to influence the contents of AD clauses of the GATT. Finger suggests that in the pitched battle between victims and users of AD laws during these negotiations, the bone of contention was the extent of AD measures that the Final Act would permit rather than ways of distinguishing socially justifiable from unjustifiable dumping. Since the determination of social justification will necessarily involve going beyond import-competing interests to include consumer-user interests, it is unlikely such weighing of all affected interests will become part of national law, let alone the GATT law.

Dispute-Settlement Procedures

Earlier I referred to Jackson's (1989) distinction between rule-oriented and power-oriented diplomacy. Abbott (1995) makes two other distinctions, between legalism and pragmatism, on the one hand, and between "private interest" and "public interest" procedures, on the other. The former distinction is self-explanatory—disputes could be resolved either by appealing to the letter of any relevant laws or by applying pragmatic considerations whether or not they are consistent with the spirit of these laws. The latter distinction is between procedures that are driven entirely by purely private interests (i.e., interests of the disputants) and those that are public-interest (i.e., systemic interest) driven. Abbott rightly argues that developing nations, having little power, would or should prefer a system that is rule-oriented, legalistic, and largely public-interest driven. However, such a system would tax the capacity of the developing country administrative apparatus by requiring trained personnel and resources to gather information and advance legal arguments.

Abbott (1995: 37) finds that the pre-UR dispute-settlement (DS) system of the GATT is almost purely private-interest oriented and that

> DS proceedings are initiated by the states affected by an alleged violation; the proceedings are controlled by those states; claims are based on the damage incurred by those states; remedies are aimed at restoring the balance of concessions between the complainant and respondent states; and sanctions take the form of retaliation by the affected state. The GATT panel is basically a passive third party; the GATT itself takes no active role in DS proceedings except perhaps to encourage settlement of the dispute.

Schott (1994: 125) adds other unsatisfactory features of the pre-UR dispute-settlement system: "overly long delays from the establishment to the conclusion of panel proceedings; the ability of disputants to block the consensus needed to approve panel findings and authorize retaliations; and the difficulty in securing compliance with panel rulings." The post-UR dispute-settlement mechanism (DSM) removes some of these flaws.

Schott (1994: 131) points out that the new mechanism

> requires the prompt establishment of panels and sets strict deadlines for their resolution of disputes. It facilitates approval of panel rulings by requiring a consensus to block reports. It establishes a new Appellate Body empowered to review panel decisions and over-rule ill-considered findings. Finally, it strengthens retaliation rights as part of improved compliance procedures, including non-automatic authority to retaliate (including cross-retaliation among sectors) if countries do not comply with panel rulings.

The new system, however, still "remains a horizontal, party-driven, private interests procedure—[it] does strengthen the private-interests procedure to a remarkable degree, ameliorating at least some of the problems faced by developing countries" (Abbott 1995: 37). The understanding with respect to the new DSM includes a number of provisions dealing specifically with cases brought by developing countries. . . . If a dispute between a developing and developed country reaches the panel stage, the former is guaranteed, on request, the presence of at least one panelist from a developing country. . . . The understanding requires [the WTO secretariat] to make available to a developing country party the assistance of a legal expert from the WTO—[also the panel] must explicitly indicate how it took account of any different or more-favorable treatment provisions in the applicable agreements that were relied upon by the developing country. (Abbott 1995: 40–41)

Other provisions take into account special problems of developing countries, and these as well as the strengthening of the DSM relative to the pre-UR situation should be a powerful tool for developing countries to enforce the commitments that the developed countries have given them.

Notwithstanding the provisions of the new DSM, the realities of disparities of power between developed and developing countries is bound to be, as Abbott suggests, the major obstacle to its increased use. I noted earlier that in the pre-UR period, there were instances when a weaker power chose not to exercise its authorization by the GATT to retaliate against a much stronger power. Abbott fears the same in the post-UR era:

Even with assistance from the Secretariat, initiating and prosecuting a case in a private-interests system will be burdensome for many developing countries, while the existence of disparate economic power may deter some from bringing complaints against major trading nations; disparate power also continues to make the ultimate sanction of retaliation—which will presumably be invoked more often than in the past under the new automatic procedures—next to meaningless for many developing countries.

It must also be borne in mind, moreover, that the same powerful, automatic procedures, including the provisions for retaliation, can and will be invoked against developing countries. There are, moreover, far fewer special provisions in the Understanding applicable to developing countries as respondents. (Abbott 1995: 41)

To sum up, the DSM of the WTO, although not free of all the problems that plagued the corresponding mechanism of the GATT, is nonetheless a substantial improvement over it. Frances Williams describes it well:

The new procedure is more rapid, more automatic and more enforceable than its predecessor in the General Agreement on Tariffs and Trade. What is most important, countries can no longer block an adverse ruling by an independent WTO dispute panel. Instead, they have the right of appeal—but the appellate body's judgment will be binding. Countries that refuse to comply will be subject to authorized trade sanctions.

Williams concludes,

> Countries are making more use of the new system than the old. Some 20 dis-
> putes have been brought to the WTO since its creation in January, far more
> than in any year of GATT's 47-year existence. Of the 16 disputes still in play,
> 15 involve one or more of the top four traders—the U.S., EU, Japan and
> Canada.
>   The WTO's ability to enforce trade judgments has also prompted devel-
> oping countries to make more use of the disputes system—launching eight
> complaints so far, including two against the U.S. and four against the EU.
> Under the GATT procedures, by contrast, powerful nations could ignore
> panel rulings with impunity and frequently did. Thus the EU brushed aside
> two GATT panels which called for changes to its banana import regime. (*Fi-
> nancial Times*, November 29, 1995: 5)

Nontariff Measures

The reductions in tariff barriers on products of major export interest to
developing countries in the Kennedy and Tokyo Rounds were lower than
the average for all products. Also, the escalation in tariffs in industrialized countries with the level of a product's processing acts as a constraint
on the export of processed rather than raw products from developing
countries. The nontariff measures (NTMs) in the OECD are considered to
be even more detrimental than tariffs to the interests of developing countries regarding their exports.

Low and Yeats (1994: 2) seek to determine "how far the Uruguay
Round, when its results are fully implemented, will change the level, nature and incidence of OECD countries' NTM's on developing countries'
exports." The major changes in NTMs brought about in the Uruguay
Round relate to "tariffication" in agriculture, the abolition of MFA, and
the elimination of voluntary export restraints, though all of these changes
will not happen instantaneously with the WTO coming into existence.
Low and Yeats find that the Uruguay Round changes will dramatically
reduce the incidence of NTMs on developing country exports, with the
share of their nonoil exports subject to NTMs falling from 18 percent to 4
percent. They caution that it is likely that industrial country producers
will demand new measures to insulate them from import competition
from developing countries that arise from the dramatic reduction of
NTMs. They suggest that safeguards and antidumping actions are the
most likely such new measures, and safeguards could indeed be invoked, albeit under restrictive conditions, to restrain imports.

7 Subregionalism, Regionalism, and Multilateralism

Richard Cooper, in his review of Kenichi Ohmae (1995), attributes to the author the view that

> modern nation-states, characterized by entrenched special interests, Olsonian distributional coalitions and rigid rules are ill-equipped to cope with a world of rapidly globalizing markets for goods and services; and ... new "region-states" of 5 million to 20 million people, possibly crossing international borders, represent the natural limits for economic growth in the future, because they are large enough to enjoy economies of scale and too small to entertain delusion of self-sufficiency. Prosperity, ... will spread from these prosperous regions to neighboring areas through trade in goods, services, capital, technology and above all, ideas "about how to prosper." (Cooper 1995: 22)

Indeed, these ideas have already taken concrete form in the development proposed for what are called "growth-triangles," such as the Singapore-Johore-Batan region (Johore is in Malaysia, Batan in Indonesia) and the Tumen River region, involving South and North Korea, China, and Mongolia. Yet as Cooper rightly argues, although growth often originates from certain regions within countries or straddles more than one country, the concept of the region-state is too amorphous to be useful; equally important, there is no way (and Ohmae offers none) by which one can identify which regions will take off or whether there are prerequisites for success beyond the willingness to open up to world competition.

Preferential trading arrangements (PTAs) among countries in a region, also called regional trading agreements (RTAs), have long been a feature of the world trading system. For example, the trade among countries of the British Commonwealth and Empire took place on a preferential basis under the system of commonwealth preferences long before the founding of the GATT. The system was in fact grandfathered into the GATT (under Article I, paragraph 2[a]) and continued for a considerable time thereafter. Other preferential arrangements covering at least a significant part, if not all, of trade include the Lomé convention, the General System of Preferences (GSP), and several others. Primarily political considerations (i.e., the concern for preventing yet another European war) led first to the formation of the European Coal and Steel Community and later to the Treaty of Rome of 1957, which established the European Community (EC). The establishment of the EC led some other European nations outside of the EC to form the European Free Trade Area (EFTA). The Soviet bloc nations created their own Council of Mutual Economic Assistance (CMEA). Inspired by the EC, several PTAs in Africa and Latin America were established in the 1960s, although not all of these were full-fledged customs unions (CUs) or even free trade areas (FTAs). Except for the EC and the EFTA, which endured, all of these arrangements collapsed sooner or later. However, the interest in regionalism revived in the late 1980s even as the UR was under way.

Between 1947 and 1994, ninety-eight RTAs were notified to the GATT under Article XXIV and a further eleven of developing countries under the Tokyo Round enabling clause (WTO 1995b: 7). But nearly half of the ninety-eight were notified during the decade 1985–1994. Since the establishment of the WTO in January 1995, twelve RTAs were notified in the area of goods, of which two involved developing countries (WTO 1995c: 17).

The most celebrated recent PTA is of course the NAFTA, signed by Canada, Mexico, and the United States in 1992 and enforced since 1994. Another is MERCOSUR, signed in 1991 by Argentina, Brazil, Uruguay, and Paraguay. The report of the Eminent Persons Group of the APEC, presented at its 1993 summit meeting, called for the establishment of an Asia-Pacific economic community with free trade and investment in the region, though the members were deeply divided about it. At their summit of 1994, APEC leaders agreed to eliminate all barriers to trade and investment in the region by 2010 in the case of developed-country members and by 2020 for others. The leaders of the Western Hemisphere in their first summit in December 1994 called for the creation of an FTA of the Americas by 2005. Chile has already been invited to negotiate its entry into NAFTA. South Asian countries have agreed on SAPTA (South Asian Preferential Trading Area), which is to become a free trade area by 2005 (brought forward to 2001 by the Male, Maldives, summit in May 1997). There is even a proposal for TAFTA, or Transatlantic Free Trade Area, which will include NAFTA (and its extensions) and the EU.

Understandably, interest in regionalism increased in the 1980s as the prospect for a successful conclusion of the Uruguay Round of multilateral trade negotiations seemed uncertain. Indeed, many (Anderson and Blackhurst 1993; Baldwin 1993; and Whalley 1993; among others) have explicitly linked the two analytically. Surprisingly, with the successful conclusion of the Uruguay Round and the establishment of the World

Trade Organization (WTO), the interest in regionalism has not waned. In fact, enthusiasm for expanding NAFTA into a hemispheric FTA and APEC into an APFTA and even for a transatlantic FTA with NAFTA and EU as members has grown. Whether such "overlapping trade agreements [are] stepping stones to global free trade—[embodying] principles of openness and inclusion consistent with the GATT" (Council of Economic Advisors 1995: 215) or, given their many economic drawbacks, they are at all "desirable when the multilateral trading system has already been jumpstarted with the ratification of the Uruguay Round by the major trading nations and the birth of the WTO" (Bhagwati 1995: 10) is a contentious issue on which distinguished economists continue to differ. Nonetheless, there is no denying that recent regionalism involves attempts at "deep integration" (see Chapter 9) going beyond the past regional PTAs in envisaging liberalization of trade in services, factor movements, harmonization of regulatory regimes, environmental and labor standards, and in fact all domestic policies perceived as affecting international competitiveness. This new regionalism has a political momentum different from that in the past. The WTO (1995b: 11) sees a complementarity between regional and multilateral integration in that members of regional agreements in certain areas have accepted higher levels of obligation than existed in earlier multilateral agreements—thus going further plurilaterally than was possible multilaterally and thereby laying the foundations for future progress multilaterally not only in those areas but also in those covered in the UR negotiations. Still, it is somewhat puzzling, if not ironic, that regionalism is being pushed at a time when developing countries are integrating with the world economy by unilaterally liberalizing their trade regimes.

Many scholars and organizations have commented on the recently revived regionalism. Their publications include, but certainly are not limited to, Anderson and Blackhurst (1993), Bhagwati (1993, 1995), Bhagwati and Panagariya (1996), Bliss (1994), De Melo and Panagariya (1993), Hufbauer and Schott (1994), Krueger (1995a), and Lawrence (1994). Many of the relevant issues have been discussed in depth in these publications.

The fundamental issue is really whether the belief of proponents of regionalism "that total trade creation will outweigh trade diversion in most cases, that the multilateral process is too slow to produce substantial progress toward further trade liberalization, and that regional free-trade arrangements will allow nations to speed up liberalization and ultimately produce a self-reinforcing process toward open markets" (Barfield 1995: vii) is simply a set of empirically testable, though as yet untested, hypotheses or whether it has acquired the status of a self-evident article of faith that needs no testing. In any case, it has become the foundation of trade policy, particularly in the United States.

In theory, a structure of common external tariffs and income transfers within a customs union of any arbitrary collection of countries can always be chosen such that no one outside the union is hurt by its formation and at least someone within the union is better off (Kemp and Wan 1976). But in the customs unions of the real world, the choice of such a globally Pareto-optimizing structure of tariffs and transfers is far from certain, if for no other reason than that the information needed to compute such a structure is unlikely to be available and the incentive compatibility problems are serious. The issue then becomes an empirical one of whether, given the composition of the unions and their tariffs and other protective measures, trade creation is likely to offset trade diversion in most cases. An FTA by definition allows each member to choose its own external tariffs, including keeping them unchanged at their pre-FTA levels so that the tariff barriers for nonmembers to its market need not be affected by the formation of the PTA. But with each member having its own external tariff, possibly at different rates, the problem of "trade deflection" arises, in which imports from a nonmember enter the member country with the lowest tariff and are transshipped to other members. To prevent it, complex rules of origin (ROOs) have to be specified. The bureaucratic complexity of ROOs and the political economy of FTAs lead Krueger (1995a) to conclude that FTAs are worse than customs unions.

Developing countries may gain higher benefits from unilaterally liberalizing all trade rather than by regionally integrating, that is, by preferentially liberalizing some of their trade (see Srinivasan and Canonero [1995] for a confirmation in the context of South Asian integration). However, from a political perspective, it might be easier to sell such liberalization as part of a *coordinated liberalization* in all the countries of a region with the liberalized access being extended to all other trading partners on an MFN basis. This idea was originally proposed by Panagariya (1994) in the context of East Asia. He found low or negative gains from subregional groupings such as the Association of Southeast Asian Nations (ASEAN), insurmountable external and internal barriers to effective integration in the case of an Asia-wide discriminatory bloc, and adverse terms-of-trade effects in the case of nondiscriminatory regionalism. He preferred the last option despite its possible adverse terms-of-trade effects, since it is more likely to promote a more liberal and open world trading system, the gains from which, in his view, will far outweigh the adverse terms-of-trade effects. However, even without coordination, it is possible that by joining a regional group (e.g., Vietnam in ASEAN) or entering into an agreement of association with a regional group (e.g., Egypt with EU), a country might engage in faster and deeper unilateral liberalization than it might otherwise do.

There are few recent analytical contributions on the issue of the process of trade liberalization (i.e., multilateral versus regional). One notable contribution is by Philip Levy (1995), who examines whether incentives for multilateral trade liberalization are blunted by the possibility of concluding regional trade agreements in a political economy model of trade policy determination. More precisely, he considers two periods; during the second, an opportunity for multilateral liberalization arises, and he asks whether two countries concluding a bilateral trade agreement in the first period will retain any interest in multilateral liberalization in the second period. In a standard Heckscher-Ohlin-Samuelson model with median voter politics, the answer is in the affirmative, since the only effect of trade liberalization, bilateral or multilateral, is the Stolper-Samuelson effect on factor prices induced by terms-of-trade changes. However, if the model is of the differentiated product–monopolistic competition type, there is an additional effect to consider, namely, an increase in the number of varieties of the product available for consumption with trade liberalization. In such a model, concluding a bilateral agreement in the first period might result in the two countries losing interest in multilateral liberalization in the second period. For example, consider two countries identical in factor endowments but differing in that respect from the rest of the world. Opening up of trade between them clearly has only a variety-expansion effect and would be beneficial. But opening up their trade with the rest of the world has both the variety-expansion and the Stolper-Samuelson effects, and these could go in opposite directions. If the negative Stolper-Samuelson effect more than offsets the variety-expansion effect, clearly the two countries would not be interested in expanding their trade bloc multilaterally.

Bhagwati (1995: 11–12) finds that

> the popular argument that free trade agreements, at least where led by the United States, will be of the "open regionalism" variety so that, with steadily increasing members, we shall arrive at full multilateralism . . . is naive for several reasons. Take the question of speed. Free Trade Agreements (FTA's) are at least as hard to negotiate as multilateral trade treaties like the Uruguay Round. After a decade, there are three countries in NAFTA; by contrast, the Uruguay Round took over seven years to negotiate, with over 115 nations and negotiations over a large range of old and new issues.

Bhagwati (1995: 13–14) concludes that

> free trade agreements become a process by which a hegemonic power seeks (and often manages) to satisfy its multiple trade-unrelated demands on other, weaker trading nations more easily than through multilateralism. The persistence of free trade arrangements despite the success of the WTO must

then be traced at least partly to an awareness of that reality. And, if this analysis has an element of truth to it, then free trade arrangements seriously damage the multilateral trade liberalization process by facilitating the capture of it by extraneous demands that aim, not to reduce barriers, but to increase them (as when market access is sought to be denied on grounds such as "eco-dumping" and "social-dumping").

Krueger (1995a: 31–32) echoes Bhagwati's dim view of FTAs:

There are a number of reasons for fearing that FTAs will push the world more toward trading blocs than toward a multilateral system. For one thing, the inherently trade-diverting aspects of FTAs suggests that their creation weakens the support of those otherwise favoring the open multilateral system, while simultaneously creating new interest groups opposing multilateral liberalization. Insofar as trade diversion does take place under FTAs, either of goods and services trade or of foreign investment, new interests will oppose further liberalization. Then, the attention of policy makers is inevitably distracted from the multilateral system when FTAs are under discussion or negotiation. Given limited resources, more attention to new FTA arrangements leaves policy makers less time to focus on the global system.

This last point is of particular concern now. When attention should center on the formation and strengthening of the new World Trade Organization, it is instead diverted to proposals for a more powerful Asia-Pacific Economic Cooperation and for new members in NAFTA. Even if, in the long run, APEC and NAFTA should evolve in ways consistent with multilateral liberalization, the distraction of attention during WTO's formative phase must surely be counted as a significant cost.

8 Trade, the Environment, and Labor Standards

Trade and the Environment

It is frequently argued that fair trade or level playing fields constitute a precondition for free trade and that therefore, harmonization of domestic policies across trading countries is necessary before free trade can be embraced to one's advantage. This argument is nowhere more manifest and compelling in its policy appeal than in the area of environmental standards.

Both the general view that cross-country intraindustry (CCII) harmonization of environmental standards is required if free trade is to be implemented and the specific proposals currently in vogue to implement this view are therefore in need of analytical scrutiny.[1] In reviewing and assessing the demands for CCII harmonization of environmental standards, it is customary to make a distinction of analytical importance between (1) environmental problems that are intrinsically *domestic* in nature; and (2) those that are intrinsically *international* in nature because they inherently involve "physical" spillovers across national borders.

Thus if India pollutes a lake that is wholly within its borders, that is an intrinsically domestic question. If, however, it pollutes a river that flows into Bangladesh, that is an intrinsically international question. So are the well-known problems of acid rain, ozone-layer depletion, and global warming. Intrinsically international problems and intrinsically domestic problems of the environment raise questions that interface with trade questions in both common and different ways.

It has become commonplace among some environmentalists to assert that this distinction is of no consequence because the intrinsically domestic environmental problems are increasingly seen to have transnational impacts. Science has shown, for instance, that aerosol sprays are not just an environmental nuisance where used; they endanger the planet! But the fact that science seems occasionally to turn local (and partial equilibrium) environmental impacts into transnational (and general equilibrium) impacts is no proof that the former are an empty set. We should not be deterred, therefore, from using this important conceptual distinction.

It would seem, at first glance, that at least the intrinsically domestic environmental problems are matters best left to governments, to domestic solutions and within domestic jurisdictions (although transnational, global "educational" and lobbying activities by environmental nongovernmental organizations, the NGOs, are compatible with this solution). If a country's preferred environmental choices and solutions (by way of setting pollution standards and taxes) to intrinsically domestic questions are different from those of another, why should anyone object to the conduct of free trade between the two on the ground that such differences are incompatible with the case for (gains from) free trade? Yet the fact is that they do.

And the objections are directed not merely at free trade but also at the institutional safeguards and practices at the WTO, which are designed to ensure the proper functioning of an open, multilateral trading system that embodies the principles of free trade. These objections take mainly four forms:

1. Unfair Trade: If you do something different, and especially if you make what appears to be less of an effort concerning the environment than I do in the same industry or sector, this is considered to be tantamount to the lack of "level playing fields" and therefore amounts to "unfair trade" by you. Free trade, according to this doctrine, is then unacceptable, as it requires as a precondition "fair trade."

2. Loss of Higher Standards: Then again, the flip side of the "fair trade" argument is the environmentalists' fear that if free trade occurs with countries having "lower" environmental standards, no matter what the justification is for this situation, the effect will be to lower environmentalists' own standards. This will follow from the political pressure brought to bear on governments to lower standards to ensure the survival of their industry.

An associated argument is that capital will move to countries with lower standards, so that countries will engage in a "race to the bottom," each winding up with lower standards than desired because standards are lowered to attract capital from each other.

3. Conflicting Ethical Preferences: Environmentalists also often want at times to impose their ethical preferences, considered "morally superior," on other nations. Free trade in products that offend one's moral sense (either in themselves or because of the way in which they are produced, as in the use of purse-seine nets in catching tuna or leghold straps in hunting for fur) is then considered objectionable because *either* trade in such

products should be withheld so as to induce or coerce acceptance of such preferences *or* such trade should be abandoned, even if it has no effective consequence and might even hurt only oneself, simply because "one should have no truck with the devil."

The former argument presumes a higher morality that should be spread to other nations with a lower morality (and with a corresponding lack of standards and laws). The latter argument seeks no such morally imperial outreach; it simply wants no part in complicity with lower morality elsewhere via participating in gainful free trade with nations guilty of tolerating such lower morality. In either case, the diversity of standards is considered to be incompatible with the pursuit of free trade.

4. Institutional Vulnerability of High Standards to Countries with Low Standards Fearing Protectionism: Finally, the environmentalists fear that they will lose their high standards not because market forces under free trade bias the domestic political equilibrium in favor of lower standards or generate a race to the bottom but because the current institutional arrangements, at the WTO in particular, enable the low-standards countries to object to and threaten the high standards in other countries by, for instance, claiming protectionist intent or consequences.[2]

Just consider why the first argument, concerning unfair trade as a result of lower CCII standards elsewhere, has become such a politically salient issue today. It should suffice to note here that the fear is that competition will be greater if a rival abroad faces lower burdens of environmental regulations. Hence the argument follows that this competitive advantage enjoyed by one's foreign rivals is illegitimate and must be countervailed, much like dumping or subsidization is, or must be eliminated at the source.

Thus former senator David Boren introduced legislation in the U.S. Congress to countervail the "social dumping" allegedly resulting from lower standards abroad, proposing such a measure on the ground that some U.S. manufacturers, such as the U.S. carbon and steel alloy industry, spend as much as 250 percent more on environmental controls as a percentage of gross domestic product than producers do in other countries. He saw in this difference an "unfair advantage enjoyed by other nations exploiting the environment and public health for economic gain."[3]

Environmental diversity among countries is, contrary to these assertions, perfectly legitimate. It can arise not merely because the environment is differently valued in the sense that the utility function defined for consumption and pollution abatement is not identical and homothetic but also because of differences in endowments and technology across countries. In fact, even with homothetic preferences, income matters: At the same cost of abatement relative to consumption, a country with ten times the income of another will spend ten times as much on abatement.

Forcing the poor country to spend as much on abatement will reduce its welfare substantially. Hence the common presumption driving demands to harmonize standards or (alternatively) to countervail the "social dumping" consequences of lower standards—that is, the assumption that others with different CCII standards are illegitimately and unfairly reducing their costs—is untenable.

Nonetheless, these demands are part of a general shift to demand harmonization of a great and possibly increasing number of domestic policies, for example, labor standards and technology policy. With industries everywhere increasingly open to competition, thanks precisely to the postwar success in dismantling trade barriers, with multinationals spreading technology freely across countries through direct investments, and with capital freer than ever to move across countries, producers now face the prospect that their competitive advantage is fragile and that more industries than ever before are "footloose." There is therefore much more sensitivity to any advantage that one's rivals abroad may enjoy in world competition and a propensity to look over their shoulders to find reasons that their advantage is "unfair."

It can be shown (Bhagwati and Srinivasan 1996), however, that the arguments in favor of free trade and diversity of environmental standards across countries is essentially robust. This follows from a straightforward extension of the proposition that under standard assumptions ensuring perfect competition in all relevant markets, free trade is globally Pareto-optimal. Introduction of environmental externalities (domestic and international) necessitates the use of appropriate taxes, subsidies, and transfers to internalize the externality but does not call for a departure from free trade to achieve a globally Pareto-optimal outcome. Still, some policy problems do arise in the context of transborder externalities.

Transborder externalities are generally more complex in character than the ones that arise with purely domestic pollution and are more compelling as well. It may be useful, from a policy viewpoint, to distinguish among two cases: (1) a special case where the problem is simplified by assuming a single country that pollutes the other, raising questions of response such as the use of trade barriers by the other; and (2) a general case where the problem is truly global in character. A good example of the former is U.S. transmission of acid rain to Canada; an excellent example of the latter is global warming, to which many countries contribute, although all are affected by it (though each in different degrees and not all negatively).

The case of one-way transmission of pollution and two countries is helpful because it illustrates in a simple way the problem raised by transborder externalities concerning the use of second-best trade instruments by the injured country when the offending country does not implement a

first-best solution and uses its jurisdictional autonomy in the spirit of ma-
lign neglect. The principal question, then, is whether a country that is being damaged by pollution from another has the right to impose a trade
restraint to affect the exports and hence the production and hence also
the pollution of the other country that comes into one's area. Modifying
the WTO rules to explicitly allow for such a possibility arguably makes
sense as a "second-best" solution, since the offending party refuses to undertake a "first-best" solution, provided the usual caveats about satisfy-
ing science tests and so on are taken into account.

The problem, of course, is that this type of trade remedy is generally
likely to be so weak for problems like acid rain that one may ask, Is it
worth modifying the WTO to legitimate such trade actions? For example,
in the United States, the generation of acid rain, a fraction of which falls
on Canada, is geographically concentrated, of course, at the border,
whereas a Canadian import tariff on U.S. products produced with electricity would affect all electricity generation in the United States. Moreover, the effect on SO_2 generation would be indirect, not direct through a
tax on the process of electricity production itself. Then again, such a tariff
would affect only a fraction of the transmission of acid rain. The tariff instrument would then be extremely weak, and the Canadian gain from its
use in reducing the loss from the acid rain would be outweighed by the
reduced gains from trade, that is, the gains from importing cheaper products from the United States. Even apart from this consideration, once a
trade policy remedy is contemplated for an environmental problem, it
will be advocated for other problems—alleged human rights violations,
endangered species, threats to biodiversity, and more ad infinitum! It will
be seized by all who want protection, and this danger of sliding down a
slippery slope is real.

The chief questions concerning trade policy when global pollution
problems such as ozone-layer depletion and global warming are involved instead take a different turn related to the cooperative-solution-
oriented multilateral treaties that are sought to address them. They are
essentially tied into noncompliance ("defection") by members and "free
riding" by nonmembers. Because any action by a member of a treaty relates to targeted actions (such as reducing CFCs or CO_2 emissions) that
are a public good (in particular, that have nonexcludable benefits such
that if I incur the cost and take an action, I cannot exclude you from benefiting from it), the use of trade sanctions to secure and enforce compliance automatically turns up on the agenda.

At the same time, the problem is compounded because the agreement
itself has to be legitimate in the eyes of those accused of free riding or
noncompliance. Before those pejorative epithets are applied and punish-
ment prescribed in the form of trade sanctions is legitimated at the WTO,

these nations have to be satisfied that the agreement being pressed on them is efficient and, especially, that it is equitable in burden-sharing. Otherwise, nothing prevents the politically powerful (i.e., the rich nations) from devising a treaty that puts an inequitable burden on the politically weak (i.e., the poor nations) and then using the cloak of a "multilateral" agreement and a new WTO legitimacy to impose that burden with the aid of trade sanctions with a clear conscience, invoking the white man's burden to secure the white man's gain.

This is why alteration of the WTO to legitimate trade sanctions (whenever a plurilateral treaty on a global environmental problem dictates it) against WTO contracting parties who remain outside of a treaty is unlikely to be accepted by the poor nations without safeguards to prevent unjust impositions. The spokespeople of the poor countries have been more or less explicit on this issue, with justification. And although the rich nations have often made the policy demand for such an alteration, they have also recognized the poor countries' concerns.

Thus at the Rio conference of 1992, the framework convention on climate change set explicit goals under which several rich nations agreed to emission-level-reduction targets (i.e., to return, more or less, to 1990 levels), whereas the commitments of the poor countries were contingent on the rich nations' footing the bill.

Ultimately, burden-sharing formulas related to past emissions, current income, current population, and so on are inherently arbitrary; they also distribute burdens without regard to efficiency. Economists will argue for burden-sharing dictated by cost minimization across countries and for the earth as a whole: If Brazilian rain forests must be saved to minimize the cost of a targeted reduction in CO_2 emissions in the world and the United States keeps guzzling gas because it is too expensive to reduce consumption, then so be it. But then this efficient "cooperative" solution must not leave Brazil footing the bill! Efficient solutions, with the compensation and equitable distribution of the gains from efficient solutions, make economic sense.

A step toward them is the idea of having a market in permits again, at the world level: No country may emit CO_2 without having bought the necessary permit, which is issued according to a worldwide quota. That would ensure efficiency, whereas the distribution of the proceeds from the sold permits would require a decision reflecting some multilaterally agreed-upon ethical or equity criteria (e.g., the proceeds may be used for refugee resettlement, UN peacekeeping operations, aid dispensed to poor nations by UNDP, or the World Health Organization's fight against AIDS). This type of agreement would have a legitimacy that could in turn provide the legitimacy for a WTO rule that permits the use of trade sanctions against free riders.

Trade and Labor Standards

Movements to improve the environment that governs employment and conditions of work, such as employment of women and children, hours of work, safety of the workplace, and materials handled in production, date back to early-nineteenth-century Europe.[4] Brown, Deardorff, and Stern (1996) suggest that these movements were driven primarily by ethical considerations. Although the link between labor standards and international trade was recognized by the reformers behind the movements, these authors cite Alam's (1992: 13) observation that the reformers generally took free trade as a given and desirable objective and sought to use moral suasion and international agreements to deal with differences among countries in labor standards. Indeed, the International Labor Organization (ILO) was founded as part of the implementation of the Treaty of Versailles of 1919, signed by the adversaries of World War I. In its decisionmaking bodies, workers, employers, and the state are represented. It has since been the premier organization in promoting better labor standards through international agreements and moral suasion. As Heribert Maier, its deputy director-general, points out,

> Over the past 75 years the ILO has adopted a series of conventions which set international labor standards. Through ratification, these conventions create binding obligations for member states. The conventions cover a wide range of issues in the world of work, including basic human rights such as freedom of association, the right to organize and bargain collectively, freedom from forced labor, freedom from discrimination in employment, and severe restrictions on the use of child labor. (Maier 1994: 12)

He emphasizes, rightly, that "traditionally, the ILO's principal means of action has been persuasion. On the whole, the focus of the international labor standards has been on their ratification, their inclusion into national legislation, and compliance with them in a national context" (Maier 1994: 12).

It is worth repeating that the ILO conventions were arrived at by multilateral agreement and their enforcement relied largely on the moral force motivating the conventions. No explicit sanctions, particularly sanctions in the form of withdrawal of rights of access to international markets, were envisaged against countries that either do not ratify any of the conventions or do not in practice comply with those that they have ratified.

The deceptively appealing notion that lower labor standards in a country relative to its trading partners confers on it an unfair competitive advantage was already present in the charter of the ITO. Article 7 of the stillborn ITO stated, "The members recognize that unfair labor conditions, particularly in the production for export, create difficulties in international trade, and accordingly, each member shall take whatever action may be appropriate and feasible to eliminate such conditions within its territory." Except for prohibition of trade goods made with prison labor, the articles of the GATT did not deal with labor standards. Various administrations in the United States, Democrat and Republican, proposed the inclusion of a labor standards article in the GATT, unsuccessfully as it turned out, during several rounds of the MTNs. Similar proposals have been made by political parties in national parliaments in several European countries and also in the European Parliament.

The latest demand is for the formal inclusion of a "social" clause in the mandate of the WTO that would allow restrictions to be placed on imports of products originating in countries not complying with a specified set of minimum standards. Such a demand in itself is not a surprise except in its timing, namely that it was raised *after* the painful and lengthy negotiations of the UR had been completed, almost holding the negotiated agreement hostage. The agreement was signed, but not without an understanding that the topic of labor standards could be discussed by the preparatory committee for the WTO. Of course, the fact that the demand has been raised repeatedly and that an understanding to discuss it has been arrived at does not necessarily make it legitimate. Indeed, as will be argued further on, if ethical considerations were the only factor behind this recent interest in labor standards, there would be no reason for demanding a social clause.

The late Jan Tinbergen, a recipient of the Nobel Memorial Prize in economics, pointed out long ago that in general there must be at least as many instruments of policy as there are objectives and that in achieving any objective, the policy instrument that has the most direct impact on the objective will most likely, though not always, do so at the least social cost (Tinbergen 1952, 1956). His principle applies as well to the creation of agencies that set the rules governing international economic transactions and the specification of their mandates. Thus the GATT and the UNCTAD were created as agencies specializing in issues relating to international trade; the World Bank and the IMF were designed to deal with financing long-term development and short-term stabilization, respectively. The Universal Postal Union covered postal and other matters of international communication. The Berne and Paris conventions (on patents and copyrights) and the World Intellectual Property Organization (WIPO) addressed many aspects of intellectual property rights. The ILO deals with labor issues. Clearly such specialization makes eminent sense. Loading one specialized agency with matters that fall within the purview of another, such as including a social clause in the mandate of the WTO rather than leaving labor standards within the purview of the

ILO, is not conducive to addressing them efficiently. A more efficient arrangement will leave each agency in charge of matters on which it is competent while ensuring, through mutual consultation and coordination where appropriate, that each avoids exclusive emphasis in its mandate while ignoring the other's and that the decisions of each do not conflict with those of the other.

It is true that proposals for a social clause often include a reference to the ILO. Such a reference, far from legitimizing the clause or providing a rationale for inclusion in the mandate of the WTO, in fact

> puts the Organization at this stage in a difficult situation. First, the *ILO has not yet reached a political consensus of its ILO constituents to identify clearly a core group of conventions or minimum standards—a kind of social charter—to be included in a social clause.* Second, the ILO's supervisory mechanism is based on persuasion (i.e., on voluntary compliance with freely accepted international obligations). . . . The ILO's supervisory mechanism was not designed to apply sanctions of any kind following non-compliance. (Maier 1994: 1, emphasis added)

The demand of developed countries for a social clause for enforcing a set of core standards on which there is no political consensus through the threat of trade sanctions is seen by many developing countries as driven largely by crass protectionist motives. Since increased competition from low-cost imports from developing countries imposes an adjustment cost in terms of declines in output and employment in import-competing industries of developed countries, forcing exporting countries to raise their labor standards in the expectation that their costs of production will rise will thus shift most, if not all, of the costs of adjustment to developing countries. Clearly, a social clause is nothing but a thinly veiled protectionist device in such a context.

The same set of questions that were raised and answered in the case of linkage between trade policies and environmental standards arises in the context of labor standards—to wit, does recognizing the impact of labor standards on the welfare of workers and on costs of production mean that there should be uniformity of such standards across trading nations? Put another way, is diversity in labor standards among nations legitimate? Three closely related issues of trade policy are cogent in this regard: (1) Does diversity in labor standards detract from the case of Pareto optimality of a global free trade equilibrium? (2) If, for whatever reasons, labor standards in one or more countries in a free trade equilibrium are deemed too low, is departure from free trade necessary in order to raise their standards to appropriate levels? (3) To the extent that higher labor standards imply higher costs, is a competitive "race to the bottom," in which all countries would end up with the lowest standards, inevitable?

The answer to all three questions in this case, as it was with respect to environmental standards, is no.

It would be indeed churlish to dismiss out of hand the humanitarian concern of the citizens of rich countries with high labor standards about the poor conditions of work or employment of children in developing countries. However, contrary to the belief among proponents of linking trade policies and labor standards, it is not necessarily the case that such a concern is best dealt with through linkage. First, it is not inconceivable that a country threatened with trade sanctions for failure to raise its labor standards would not respond by raising them but instead choose to forgo gains from trade. Second, instead of relying on the *indirect means* through linkage, which depends on the desired response by the developing country for its success, the citizens of the developed countries could adopt a more effective *direct means* of pressuring *their own governments* to lift any restrictions on the immigration of workers from countries with poor labor standards. If they chose to migrate, such workers would enjoy the higher labor standards prevailing in the country of immigration. Indeed, there is support for lifting such restrictions on moral-philosophical grounds, as in the writings of John Rawls (1993a). He views freedom of movement and freedom of choice of occupation as essential primary goods equivalent to other basic rights and liberties, the entitlement to which is not open to political debate and allocation through the political process. Although Rawls was writing about these freedoms in the context of constitutional essentials of a just society, implicit in the very expression of humanitarian concerns about others must be a view of the whole human race as one society. Thus a natural extension of Rawls's ideas would treat freedom of movement of humans across artificial political boundaries as a basic human right.[5] Of course, none of the proponents of linkage who wax eloquent about some labor standards as basic human rights ever raise the issue of the human right of free movement across countries.

Even if lifting immigration restrictions is deemed unfeasible politically, citizens of rich countries could make income transfers to workers in poor countries. With higher incomes, it is reasonable to presume that the *supply* price (broadly defined to include labor standards) of their labor would rise, and to restore labor market equilibrium, labor standards would have to rise. Indeed, a test of the depth of their humanitarian concern is the price that citizens are willing to pay for translating the concern into an actual increase in welfare of workers in poor countries. In fact, without transfers, imposing higher labor standards than a less developed economy can sustain could mean lower employment and welfare levels for its citizens. The willingness to make needed income transfers is a demonstration of the willingness to pay the price.

Regarding child labor, it is reasonable to presume that the welfare of their children will weigh significantly in the choices made for them by all parents except the abusive ones. In making those choices, given their resources and opportunities, parents could be reasonably expected to take into account the cost of putting their children to work in terms of their health and education relative to the income they bring in. Thus if some parents choose to put their children to work, it reflects more than anything else the limitations of their resources and opportunities, namely their poverty. Once again, citizens of developed countries concerned with the welfare of such working people in developing countries could influence the choice of parents away from putting their children to work altogether or at least reduce the amount of work done by their children through income transfers to parents. Such transfers relax their resource constraints. Again, linkage is not called for.

An alternative to income transfers other than linkage concerns the actions of citizens of developed countries in their markets for imported products. By not buying products of a firm or a country that does not observe what consumers view as acceptable labor standards, they can send a clear and effective signal to that firm or country to force it to choose between observing standards and retaining the market or losing the market altogether.[6] If it chooses to retain the market by observing acceptable labor standards, to the extent the cost of the import goes up because of such observance, both the exporting industry and buyers of imports share the cost of improving labor standards. If it chooses to forgo the market, then although workers in the exporting industry do not gain welfare through higher standards, there is a penalty to the firm in the form of lost exports. If the citizens of the developed countries are interested only in raising the welfare of the workers and not in penalizing the exporting firm, they will have to compensate the firm or make income transfers to workers. The basic point is that there is a real cost to raising labor standards, and this cost has to be incurred if the intended benefit is to come about.

It is argued that since the Uruguay Round agreement has extended the GATT disciplines to trade-related intellectual property (TRIPs) and investment measures (TRIMs), extending it to include labor standards is no less legitimate. As Bhagwati (1994) points out, the GATT rules are meant to promote economic efficiency, not to protect the interests of specific factors of production. TRIPs and TRIMs are by definition *trade related*: The transfer and diffusion of technology through licensing patented technology is trade in technology. There is no such direct link in the case of labor standards.

It can be shown (Srinivasan 1996c) that from the analytical perspective, diversity in labor standards or the implementation of common minimal standards does not call for deviation from free trade as long as Pareto optimality is the objective and there is willingness not only to make income transfers between countries as necessary but, to the extent standards in one country directly affect the welfare of another, to internalize such externalities in each country. It can also be shown that a destructive "race to the bottom" is not inevitable in the competition to set labor standards.

One of the core labor standards promoted by the ILO is the freedom of workers to form labor unions and presumably engage in collective bargaining. For an overwhelming majority of poor workers in developing countries whose dominant mode of employment is self-employment in rural agricultural activities or in the urban informal sector, unionization has little relevance. Even where relevant and where the freedom to form unions has been exercised to a significant extent, namely in the organized manufacturing and public sector in poor countries, labor unions have been promoting the interests of a small section of the labor force at the expense of many. Indeed, as the late Professor P. C. Mahalanobis, eminent Indian statistician and planner, long ago pointed out,

> certain welfare measures tend to be implemented in India ahead of economic growth, for example, in labor laws which are probably the most highly protective of labor interests in the narrowest sense, in the whole world. There is practically no link between output and renumeration; hiring and firing are highly restricted. It is extremely difficult to maintain an economic level of productivity or improve productivity. . . . In India with a per capita income of only about $70, the present form of protection of organized labor, which constitutes, including their families, about five or six percent of the whole population, would operate as an obstacle to growth and would also increase inequalities. (Mahalanobis 1969: 442)

Of course, whether or not unions promote general welfare, there is no rationale for their suppression. But it should be recognized, first, that unionized labor often constitutes a small labor aristocracy in poor countries. Second and more important, promoting labor standards that cannot be sustained in equilibrium at a particular stage of development of a country could be very expensive in terms of forgone growth. Depending on whether such standards vary across industries and the time phasing of their introduction, wage and profit rates and employment in different industries as well as in the aggregate would be affected differently. These effects would depend on the technology and the characteristics of labor standards, and no general answer can be given.

Whatever the analytical foundations for linking trade policies and labor standards, it is not a coincidence that the demand for the inclusion of a "social" clause in the mandate of the WTO is shrillest in developed countries and at the present time. After all, unemployment has been growing and real wages have been stagnant in many of these countries in a period when global economic integration has been growing and when competition from some dynamic less developed countries has been intensifying as well. It is not surprising to see the ancient but crude pauper-labor argument reappear, but now couched in lofty and idealistic terms of "fair" labor standards. Robert Reich (1994: 3), the secretary of labor in the United States, stated these arguments clearly: Producers in high-standard countries would be out-competed by those in countries that do not impose such standards and would be "forced to respond by cutting wages and benefits and working conditions in a destructive race for the bottom." Fortunately, he dismissed them by pointing out that "technological change is a much larger factor than third-world competition in the growth of low-wage work in the United States."

Several studies suggest that if we allow for productivity differences, labor is not much cheaper in many of the developing countries, and in any case, differences in unit labor costs and in costs of meeting environmental regulations are not the driving forces in the locational decisions of multinational corporations. Also, as discussed earlier, there are policy instruments that are superior to trade sanctions, for example, income transfers. Such policies could serve the purpose of improving labor standards in developing countries. Even if there is an international consensus on minimum standards, as Charnovitz (1994) points out, the potential for its capture by protectionists is significant. A social clause would be used for not only gaining protection but also enunciating basic labor standards, and monitoring their observance would become yet another avenue for "managed trade." It is likely that if the social clause is incorporated in the mandate of the WTO, it will disrupt the healthy growth in international trade along the lines of comparative advantage and retard the development of poor countries and, thereby, their progress toward a better life for their workers and their families. Monitoring the observance of standards could lead to managed trade and intrusion into the domestic political processes of other countries. Indeed, Secretary Reich (1994: 5) appeared to suggest precisely such an intrusion when he said, "If a country lacks democratic institutions *and* fails to disseminate the benefits of growth, other countries might justifiably conclude that low labor standards are due not to poverty itself, but to political choices that distort development and warp the economy's structure."

Unfortunately, in the real world, even as the trend is distinctly toward some form of democratic government, the sad fact is that a very large proportion of the world's population is ruled by governments in the choice of which they have little to say. Even where elections for such choice are regularly held and some basic political and social rights of citizens are formally guaranteed in constitutions, the participation of particular groups in the population in elections is restricted by other economically or socially powerful groups, often by threats of violence. The guarantee of rights is often not enforced because the government is too weak or too resource-constrained and sometimes not enforced because the government chooses otherwise. Further, in almost all international institutions, nations constitute the membership, and the ruling government represents each nation. Under these circumstances, the "first best," that is, a situation in which governments reflect the preferences of a majority—because it has had ample opportunities to express its own preferences freely in the democratic process and has enough political and economic instruments at its command to enforce any international agreements into which it freely enters—does not obtain. Also, the labor standards that prevail (for example, with respect to workers' freedom of association to form unions of their choice or with respect to occupational safety or child labor) may not have the legitimacy of having been the outcome of a democratic social-political-economic process.

It is tempting to conclude that in a world that is far from the "first best," consultations with and suasion of governments, as practiced by the ILO, to ensure the observance of commonly agreed-upon standards (such as freedom of association in the establishment of unions) are bound to be ineffective and that governments will selectively comply with those agreements that they find in their interest and ignore others. Thus linkage in the sense of denying the benefits of agreements (e.g., market-access privileges on a most-favored-nation basis for the WTO members) that a government chooses to abide by is likely to be far more effective in forcing it to comply with the provisions of other agreements (e.g., ILO consensus on some labor standards) and to abandon violating the basic human rights of some or all of its citizens.

A commonly claimed example of the successful use of trade sanctions is those sanctions used against South Africa to force its government to abandon apartheid. Without getting into the question of whether in fact trade sanctions played other than a minor supporting role in the collapse of apartheid[7] and into far more numerous examples (Hufbauer, Schott, and Elliott 1990a, 1990b) of failed trade sanctions and embargoes, I feel it suffices to say that first, except in the context of proven and willful violation of some universally agreed-upon basic principle or right, formalizing the use of sanctions has to be approached with extreme caution. Such a universal agreement does not exist with respect to many labor and environmental standards. Second, even worse than the dangers of possible misuse of the threat of sanctions is the near certainty that such threats will encourage the unilateral exercise of the threat of sanctions by powerful countries against the weak because they find it time consuming and irksome to persuade others to go along in imposing multilateral actions.

The unilateralism exercised by the United States through Section 301 or Super 301 provisions of its domestic trade laws in matters that were either in the province of the dispute-settlement procedures of the GATT or were not part of any international agreements should serve as a warning in this regard.

It is rather ironic that the U.S. secretary of labor questions the political choices with respect to labor standards made by governments of countries without functioning democratic institutions. In all of the four decades of cold war, the political decisions of governments that chose to be on the side of the so-called free world were accepted and applauded without any questions of the existence of functioning democratic institutions in them ever being raised! Be that as it may, ultimately any challenge to the government of a nation that is not initiated by that nation's citizens but is the result of external sanctions will not be seen as legitimate by the citizenry in general and is unlikely to be successful regardless of the desirability of the objectives of imposers of sanctions. This is not to devalue the significance of external opprobrium—indeed, it might even encourage citizens to challenge the legitimacy of their government's actions, if not that of governments themselves. Indeed, the consensus approach of the ILO and its consultative and assistance (technical and other) mechanisms that attempt to persuade and help national governments enforce standards are more likely, though not absolutely certain, to make a resisting government lose the support of its own citizens.[8] And the sanctions imposed with such a sledgehammer of a social clause in the WTO would almost surely unite the same citizens behind their governments in resisting what would be seen as foreign bullying!

Notes

This chapter is based on Bhagwati and Srinivasan (1996).

1. CCII means harmonization of standards within the same industry across different trading countries.

2. The difficulties posed by the WTO for the environmentalists extend to WTO legal procedures, that is, dispute-settlement-panel findings, in regard to the ethical-preference issue as well.

3. David L. Boren, *International Pollution Deterrence Act of 1991*, Senate Finance Committee, October 25, 1995.

4. This section is based on Srinivasan (1996c).

5. By accepting existing political boundaries, Rawls himself does not make such an extension in his essay "Law of Peoples" (Rawls 1993b) and is criticized for this failure by Ackerman (1994). In his earlier work, Ackerman (1971: 89–95, 256–257) argued that although there may be some grounds for restriction on immigration in real-world states, such restrictions not only should be exercised with

great care, given the ease with which they may be abused, but also must be accompanied by a massive increase in foreign aid.

6. It might appear that consumers must have the information needed to distinguish the nonobserving firms from the observing ones to engage in such behavior. However, market forces might themselves generate such information as long as the consumers refuse to buy that product (or *all* products from a country) if they suspect *some* firms (or some *products* from that country) are being produced under unacceptable conditions. In such a case, producers (or countries) who maintain acceptable standards will have an incentive to invest in signaling (in a credible way) to consumers that they in fact do so and thus distinguish themselves from those that do not.

Michiel Keyzer, in a private conversation, raised a troubling aspect of consumer boycott. Of course, boycott of products produced under working conditions that consumers deem unacceptable would seem appropriate. But how should one view boycott of products because they have been produced by particular groups in other countries that consumers in one country deem unacceptable for reasons of racial, ethnic, or other prejudices?

The EU introduced a voluntary Eco-Label scheme in 1992 under which manufacturers can apply for the label that certifies their product as environmentally satisfactory, taking into account its environmental impact during production, distribution, use, and disposal. According to Thorstensen and Peña (1997), UNCTAD (1994, 1995) found that even such voluntary schemes could have a potential for adverse trade effects for developing countries.

7. For an empirical analysis see Kaempfer and others (1992).

8. It is unfortunate that the director-general of ILO seems to want the ILO to go beyond its traditional consensus approach and toward a more coercive one. I comment on this in Chapter 12.

9 Making the Best out of the Post–Uruguay Round World: Institutional Innovations and Reforms in Developing Countries

Stephan Haggard (1995: 2) defines integration as "the fundamentally political process of policy coordination and adjustment designed to facilitate closer economic interdependence, and to manage externalities that arise from it." Haggard and other contributors to the Project on Integrating National Economies of the Brookings Institution distinguish between "shallow" and "deep" integration. "Shallow" integration involves the relaxation of interventions at national borders on trade and investment. "Deep" integration may be induced once "shallow" integration is substantially completed. It involves coordination at a minimum, and complete harmonization at a maximum, of domestic institutions and policies that are deemed to affect international competition. Three targets of "deep" integration currently on the agenda of international negotiations are identified by Haggard as relevant from the perspective of developing countries: differences in policy measures that relate to foreign investment; differences in national regulatory regimes with respect to their financial and industrial sectors, including in particular, rules governing intellectual property, technology transfer, and environmental standards; differences in national, corporate, and political structures insofar as they are perceived as restraints on trade and investment. Although TRIMs, TRIPs, and services parts of the Uruguay agreement dealt with some of these issues, clearly, many have yet to reach the state of formal international agreement. For example, the Committee on Trade and the Environment in the WTO, which has met several times since its establishment, has focused on the issues of exports of domestically prohibited goods, transparency, and dispute settlement and on TRIPs, services, and the relationship between environmental policies related to trade and environmental measures with significant trade effects and the provisions of the multilateral trading system. But as yet, the committee has not made any recommendations for the consideration of WTO's decisionmaking bodies. However, the absence of international agreements does not mean that developing countries will not be under some pressure to act on some of the issues.

Whether "deep" integration is genuinely in the interest of developing countries and whether "shallow" integration is a precondition for deep integration are analytically unsettled issues. Dani Rodrik (1995) points out in his comments on Krueger (1995b) that economists know much less about the desirability of "deep" integration than the desirability of "shallow" integration, and what is even more serious, their analytical framework is ill-equipped to think about "deep" integration. Yet he argues that despite its substantial downside risk, deep integration has considerable upside potential as well for the developing countries. But realizing this potential, and indeed reaping the known and substantial benefits of shallow integration following the Uruguay agreement, will call for major institutional innovations and thoroughgoing reforms in many developing countries.

Clearly, the enormous diversity among developing countries in their institutional and economic development matters in realizing the gains from integrating with the global economy, at least in the short and medium runs. For example, for a country in which subsistence production dominates economic activity and transport and in which the communication infrastructure is either poor or nonexistent, the fact that the external trading and investment environment has become more liberal with the conclusion of the UR agreement may not mean much. Given its stage of development, by acceding to WTO and subscribing to its rules, it can gain very little. At the other end of the spectrum, for an advanced developing country that has already completed "shallow" integration and has a well-developed infrastructure and functioning institutions, deeper integration is not only feasible but also essential for its growth. Indeed, Krueger (1995b) cites the accession into the EU of Portugal and Spain as an example of the feasibility of deep integration on a phased-in time schedule once shallow integration and other reforms have been in process for a reasonable time. Clearly, the experience of Portugal and Spain is relevant not only for Turkey, whose entry into a customs union with the EU has been approved, but also for other advanced developing countries in Asia and Latin America.

Even though there is an enormous diversity of developing countries, two broad areas in which reforms and changes in existing institutions or the creation of new institutions would be needed can be identified: administration, narrowly construed, and economy-wide (indeed society-wide) systems. Many of the institutional changes needed in order to reap the maximum benefits from the post-UR environment for trade and investment are also needed for the success of economic liberalization and reforms under way in many developing countries. This is certainly the case with administrative reforms. As Krueger (1995b: 64) rightly remarks, "Policy reform is not, therefore, simply a process of changing one or two aspects of governmental regulations and behaviors, it requires fairly stringent reorientation of government agencies away from 'control' and 'policing' functions and toward provision of public services and a level playing field for private economic activity."

The experience of the World Bank with policy reform also led to a similar conclusion. As Ernest Stern, the former managing director of the bank and the architect of its structural adjustment lending, put it in his introduction to Thomas and others (1991: 3),

> In general, it is fair to say, we grossly underestimated the institutional elements of adjustment at both the macro and sectoral levels. Time and again the best of policy intentions, the best of policy letters solemnly agreed to and signed by the finance minister and the Bank, broke down. This often happened because of a lack of adequately trained people in the right places, the difficulty of changing bureaucratic structures, and the difficulty of laying people off as functions were reduced.

The same refrain is repeated in other chapters of his book that deal with reforms of particular sectors of the economy.

A system of economic management based on "control" exercised at their discretion by politicians and administrators almost invariably creates opportunities for a "corrupt" exercise of power. At the same time, because of the premium associated with being able to influence the discretionary decisions of those with power and also because of the often opaque, lengthy, and time-consuming process of applying for needed administrative permissions, a class of middlemen who "facilitate" the process for a consideration by using their contracts and knowledge of the system emerges. Moving away from such a system to one based on clear rules and procedures, applied in a transparent and impartial way, means a redistribution of power and income within the society. Stern asserts that those at the World Bank and everyone else "underestimated the political difficulty of adjustment [and] we failed to give full weight in our own thinking to the fact that structural adjustment means a major redistribution of economic power and hence of political power" (Thomas et al. 1991: 4). I would also draw attention to the direction of causation going the other way—from redistribution of political power (in the broad sense of power over administrative decisions affecting the income and wealth of the population) to redistribution of economic power. In many developing countries, the pursuit of state-directed, capital-intensive, import-substituting strategies of industrialization redistributed political power, and hence economic power, away from producers of exportables and labor toward producers of importables, owners of capital as well as bureaucrats and politicians. Structural adjustment and trade liberalization naturally involves reversing this earlier redistribution.

Apart from the redistribution of power, there is the practical issue of designing administrative procedures, norms, rules, and so on. First, greater transparency and insulation from politics of decisionmaking on trade and foreign investment issues should be achieved by establishing *technical and quasi judicial* bodies for making recommendations to the government on them. For example, a trade and industry commission could be entrusted with assessing proposals for foreign investment, relief from import competition, complaints of dumping, and other issues. The commission would hold public hearings in which all affected interests (including foreign interests) would have an opportunity to present their case. Commissioners would be experienced professionals. The conception of Japan's MITI (Ministry of International Trade and Industry) as an omniscient and omnipotent agency that is solely responsible for Japan's rise to economic superpower status has led some to suggest going further and establishing a powerful agency to coordinate the decisions of all economic ministries. Whether or not MITI indeed was responsible for Japan's growth, the centralization of decisions in a single agency is unlikely to be of help in most developing countries.

The reforms often involve "contracting out" to the private sector of activities, such as construction of roads and other public works, previously directly executed by the public sector. Such a shift, to be effective, has to ensure that there is adequate competition among private contractors and appropriate and transparent procedures for the evaluation and award of contracts. To take another example, the reform of the financial sector often involves removing controls on lending and deposit rates and drastically reducing the volume of "directed" credit, that is, credit allocated in such volume and terms and to such sectors (or maybe even to specified borrowers) as directed by the government. Clearly, when the interest rates are controlled and the volume of funds either appropriated by the government to itself at zero interest through various reserve requirements or directed by the government to be lent on specified terms forms an overwhelming proportion of the deposit base, the banks, whether public or private, have little room to choose among alternative lending opportunities. But once the reforms are in place, the banks must acquire the capacity to evaluate the risks and return from alternating lending opportunities and, particularly over the longer term, to gather the information needed for such an evaluation and to institute procedures for making evaluations routine. Also, as the experience with financial deregulation in industrialized countries amply demonstrates, appropriate prudential regulations on banks and other financial intermediaries are essential if they are to operate responsibly in a deregulated environment.

The next example involves the creation of research capacity and institutional structures for managing inflows of external capital, particularly of volatile portfolio investment. With the opening up of large economies, such as Brazil, China, and India, that were earlier closed to foreign investment, the volume of private capital flowing to them has increased. On the one hand, such flows, if not sterilized by the central bank, can lead to an appreciation of the exchange rate and a consequent loss of international competitiveness. On the other hand, if they are sterilized, domestic interest rates might rise, attracting even more inflows. Besides, given the substantial volatility of such flows, an adverse shock (*not necessarily* to the "fundamentals" of the economy) could trigger massive outflows. An appropriate level of exchange reserves, along with access to credit to accommodate such outflows, is needed if a disruptive change in the exchange rate is to be avoided. Analyzing how much, if any, of the inflows are to be sterilized and calculating the "appropriate" level of reserves (and the amount of credit to be held in reserve) are issues that would be challenging even to the best-trained and experienced decision-makers at the central bank. Whether the central bank can sterilize at all in large part depends on the market for government debt. If the amount of privately held stock of public debt is relatively small and a secondary market for debt is absent, sterilization by the central bank through open market operations is unfeasible.

The last example relates to the privatization of public enterprises. Some of the enterprises proposed to be privatized often have a significant share of the market for their product or may even be monopolies (for example, public utilities such as electric power companies). In such cases or more generally in cases where adequate market competition among private enterprises is unlikely, a framework of regulation of the market behavior of private firms has to be established prior to privatization.

As mentioned earlier, domestic regulatory policies are likely to move into the areas of international negotiations under the rubric of competition policies in the next round of the MTNs under the WTO. Scherer (1994: 92) has already proposed the creation of an *international competition policy office* within the ambit of the WTO. The developing countries, which already have a regulatory framework or are about to design one as part of their reforms, are likely to come under pressure.

An area of economy-wide and systemic significance in which innovation and reform are needed in the post-UR world is the legal system and, more broadly, the constitutions of some developing countries. Needless to say, as the role of the market expands and foreign suppliers and investors are viewed with enthusiasm rather than suspicion, commercial laws have to be streamlined and made transparent. The cost in terms of time and resources needed not only to meet the legal requirements of setting up an establishment or of floating equities or selling commercial paper in the domestic financial markets but also to settle any commercial disputes has to be reduced. In some of the so-called transition economies, in which experience with the market economy is a distant memory and where rights to private ownership of the means of production was abolished long ago, the task of creating an appropriate legal framework is much broader and more complex than in the mixed economies of many developing countries.

There are two other sets of laws that need to be examined from the perspective of their potentially being major constraints on the economic liberalization process. These are bankruptcy and labor laws. In some of the larger developing countries (e.g., India) in which the public sector was assigned a dominant role in the strategy of development and was also expected to be a "model" employer, the laws were designed to make it extremely costly for an enterprise in either the public or the private sector to go bankrupt. Indeed, those private enterprises that were no longer profitable were taken over by the public sector and often run at greater losses, primarily to ensure the continued employment of their workers. Clearly, privatization cannot go very far in such a context without a reform of bankruptcy laws.

Laws governing the hiring, firing, job security, wages, fringe benefits, and so on of workers in many developing countries have been enacted in imitation of those that are on the statute books of much richer, developed countries. These do not reflect the economic realities of their own labor markets. A "labor aristocracy" consisting of an extremely small proportion of the total labor force employed in the organized manufacturing and the public sector, including public administration, enjoys the benefits conferred by such laws, and the bulk of the labor force has no access to such benefits. Such laws, if effectively enforced, raise labor costs beyond what they would have been in an equilibrium of the labor market with laws in consonance with the stage of development of the country. These have to be drastically amended, if not repealed, for such countries to reap the maximum benefits from a liberalized world market for labor-intensive manufactures in which they are likely to have a comparative advantage.

The effects of the changed global economic environment after many developing countries liberalized their foreign trade and investment and after the conclusion of the UR are already evident in many spheres. Two are particularly noteworthy. Flows of portfolio investment (particularly from institutional investors in developed countries) to some developing countries have increased significantly. A scramble is also under way from foreign investors, including multinationals, to get a piece of the huge investment in infrastructure (particularly power transport and telecommunication) that many developing countries (including China and India) are to undertake. A number of institutional innovations and reforms are needed to ensure that developing countries benefit from such flows and investment and avoid some of the inherent pitfalls.

The innovations needed for enhancing the capacity of the central bank to manage the impact of foreign capital inflows were pointed out earlier. Both managing portfolio flows and borrowing in world capital markets by domestic firms through the so-called global depository receipts require setting up (if none exist) institutions for the regulation of markets for financial securities as well as reforming transactions procedures in such markets. In some developing countries, ostensibly to prevent what is deemed to be destructive speculation and speculative bubbles, formal futures trading is prohibited. Of course, this does not prevent such trading from taking place informally. Once we have reformed financial markets, established prudential norms, and created appropriate regulatory institutions, whether banning future trading or, for that matter, restricting the creation and sale of new financial products (including derivatives) makes sense has to be evaluated. It was noted earlier that the safeguards mechanisms in the WTO make it easier to invoke antidumping measures. In hitherto inward-oriented economies with high-cost industries that are profitable only behind protective walls, liberalization may result in a surge in imports. In such economies, it might be tempting, even necessary, to enact antidumping laws and use them. However, there is always the danger that such laws, once enacted, could be put to inappropriate uses.

In this context, some features specific to foreign direct investment in infrastructure have to be kept in mind. Such investments usually involve sizable chunks of capital, are lumpy, and take several years to complete, and their output is likely to be sold in markets that are regulated. These features imply that there are likely to be few potential projects undertaken in a country within any reasonable time horizon, and a consortium rather than a single investor might have to be involved in financing a project. Last and most important, failing to conclude an agreement to invest and starting project construction can create shortages in the future, since most infrastructural services cannot be imported. The visibility and size of projects and the fact that only a few projects can be undertaken also imply that the intrusion of politics into the decisionmaking on which projects to fund cannot be easily avoided.

The recent episode relating to the biggest foreign investment ever in India in the state of Maharashtra illustrates many of the problems. The investment was by Enron, an American company, to build and operate a power plant costing $2.8 billion. It had been approved by the state government then in power and the central government. The investor in effect had been guaranteed a rate of return of 16 percent by the central government, and the price at which power was to be sold by the company to the state's electricity board was also fixed in the contract. The contract was negotiated with Enron alone; no competitive bidding was called for under India's fast-track procedure for negotiations with foreign investors in power projects. This procedure was meant to enlarge electricity-generating capacity rapidly so as to compensate for large anticipated shortfalls in the power supply. The newly elected state government canceled the contract, alleging (so far unproved) bribery by Enron and also objected to the high price that Enron was to be paid for its supply of power. As the *Economist* (August 12, 1995: 27–28) put it, "In the absence of competitive bidding, there was scope for cost-padding and crony capitalism. Accusations of corruption were inevitable, justified or not, and Enron's project bore the brunt, being the biggest of seven such projects, and the first." The *Economist* also reported that "the central government has now wisely changed its power policy and decreed competitive bidding for future projects" (p. 28). Enron and the state government have since negotiated the terms, with Enron agreeing to scale down the price of power to lower the capital costs. Construction has resumed, and the project is likely to come on stream as or even earlier than originally scheduled. Enron has even expressed interest in investing in other projects. There is no doubt that had the project been abandoned, there would have been a significant shortfall in the future power supply, a shortfall that could not be eliminated, since there are no alternative projects that are approved and ready to be implemented.

It goes without saying that inviting competitive bids, evaluating them, and then awarding a contract in a way that is transparent and precludes collusion and rigging in the bidding process requires institutional and analytical capabilities that few developing countries are likely to have. Although a vigilant and free press and transparency of procedures would certainly help reduce, if not prevent, political and administrative corruption in the awarding of contracts, resisting pressure, not often very subtle, by foreign governments is another matter, particularly when the government applying pressure is a powerful one.

For example, the U.S. government announced (in 1993)

> the establishment of a new commercial strategy focusing on the overseas markets that hold the most promise for U.S. exports and investment over the long term. We selected ten economies, designated the Big Emerging Markets (BEMs), and designed a strategy aimed at encouraging commercial cooperation with the BEMs and helping U.S. firms seize the opportunities the markets offer. (Letter from President Clinton in U.S. Department of Commerce 1995)

The ten BEMs are Argentina, Brazil, ASEAN (now including Vietnam), the Chinese Economic Area (China, Hong Kong, and Taiwan), India, Mexico, Poland, South Africa, South Korea, and Turkey. The introduction to the BEMs study clearly states that in each of the markets

> competition will be fierce. But, because many have important state sectors and because virtually all are focusing heavily on infrastructure projects that demand involvement of local governments U.S. companies will need the U.S. government *at their side to win a fair hearing*. What is more, because of the intensity of foreign competition and the capital demands on these economies, our competitors will be public-private partnerships in which foreign governments are providing concessionary financing and *aggressive advocacy* to support their companies' efforts. If we don't do the same, we will lose not only our chance to succeed in these markets but our chance to re-main the world's largest economic leader in the next century. (U.S. Depart-ment of Commerce 1995: 18–19, emphasis added)

The study goes on to identify the role and policies of the U.S. govern-ment in promoting U.S. interests in BEMs:

> There is an important role for our government to play in helping to stimulate our trade with each of the BEMs. The BEMs are unlike our more traditional trading partners, such as Great Britain or Germany. There are frequently se-vere barriers to entering these markets, including high tariffs, quotas and protectionist regulatory restrictions. Commercial systems, including full re-spect for intellectual property rights, smoothly functioning capital markets and open government procurement procedures, are often still developing or lacking altogether. In some of the BEMs, impartial legal systems are missing, too. And as noted earlier, the nature of the competition we face in these mar-kets is dramatically different from what we have been used to.
> In these markets, therefore, we can and should help American businesses in a variety of ways from securing market access to providing financing to supporting U.S. companies seeking to win major projects on deals in which foreign governments are helping their firms or play an important decision-making role in awarding projects. (U.S. Department of Commerce 1995: 22)

One would hope that a representative of the government in any one of the BEMs, in negotiating with a representative of an American enterprise that has the aggressive support of the U.S. government, will not be intim-idated into conceding too much. It is reasonable to presume that govern-ments of major industrial countries would be supporting their compa-nies in their negotiations with governments in BEMs as well as in other developing countries. Often, in a context of costly and asymmetric infor-mation, foreign companies and their governments are likely to have a better information base and analytical support compared with their domestic counterparts. In such a situation, the developing-country negotiators will be at a disadvantage.

Constitutional reforms are also needed in some of the large developing economies. In such economies, which have several layers of government with different responsibilities, resources, and administrative capabilities, a reform process initiated at the central level could prove ineffective if the state- or provincial-level government either is not convinced of the need for reform or is less administratively capable. How the tax base is allocated between the layers of government, whether the system of fiscal transfers from the center to the states is compatible with each state doing its best in mobilizing resources, and whether all layers have equal access to domestic capital and credit markets are issues that have to be addressed.

In China in the recent past, the provincial governments were able to be fiscally expansive by borrowing from the banking system because the central bank had not exercised a firm control over such credit creation. In many developing countries, central banks do not have the independence and autonomy to restrain the fiscal authorities by refusing to monetize excessive fiscal deficits. To the extent the independence of a central bank provides an assurance to external investors that inflation will be restrained and the power to intervene in financial (including foreign exchange) markets will be exercised infrequently and responsibly, clearly foreign capital flows will be encouraged by such independence. Constitutionally mandated independence will be more credible than statements by the government that it will not influence the central bank's policymaking.

Many of the institutional reforms, if designed properly and implemented effectively, will call for the training of administrators and policymakers at various levels in developing countries. The IMF and the World Bank provide several training courses of this kind. Other regional banks and the UN system also provide training. To my knowledge, the courses and training do not cover alternative legal systems (particularly with respect to commercial laws) and alternative ways of decentralizing tax and administrative systems in constitutional law. Also, more thought should be given to putting together an analytically coherent typology of member countries based on their institutional development and other relevant factors. After all, not all countries will need the same set of training courses, and not all of the new institutions (particularly with respect to analysis and information gathering) need to be national. Designing national, regional, and broader institutions to enable developing counties to take full advantage of the emerging opportunities and at the same time ensure that they have a say in global decisionmaking is an urgent task.

To sum up, although major domestic institutional reforms and investment in physical and social infrastructure will be needed for many developing countries to take full advantage of the opportunities opened up by the UR agreement, this does not mean that they should wait until these reforms and investments are in place before attempting to integrate their economies with the global economy. On the contrary, they should go ahead with such integration: The domestic constraints could reduce but not eliminate the benefits from integration.

Notes

I have drawn on Srinivasan (1996b) in writing this chapter.

10 Cooperation Among the Multilateral Economic Institutions

The architects of the post–World War II international economic institutions had intended the so-called Bretton Woods twins, the IMF and the World Bank, to be complemented by the International Trade Organization (ITO). For the reason described in Chapter 2, the ITO did not come into being and the GATT, though technically not an international organization, partially substituted for the missing ITO. With the collapse of the Bretton Woods system of fixed exchange rates in the early 1970s, the role of the IMF in sustaining a stable exchange-rate system disappeared. In fact, even prior to the 1970s the contribution of the IMF's monitoring and enforcement toward sustaining the system was relatively modest. For instance, Kahler (1995: 5) points to the fact that "major countries often changed their exchange rate without notifying the IMF—Canada floated its exchange rate from 1950 to 1960, and the IMF imposed no sanctions. The record on multiple exchange rates was equally spotty—as late as 1962, fifteen of eighty two members of the IMF had multiple rates." With exchange rates of major currencies floating and each country becoming free to choose its own exchange-rate regime and with mutual recognition of such freedom, Article IV of the IMF was amended, obliging members only to "collaborate with the Fund and other members to assure orderly exchange arrangements and to promote a stable system of exchange rates." The IMF's role in overseeing these obligations was captured in the concept of surveillance. Narrowly defined, it encompassed scrutiny of exchange-rate policies; more broadly defined, it extended the fund's monitoring to include domestic policies (Kahler 1995: 54). But as Kahler notes, unless a member requested financial support from the IMF, the new surveillance procedures appeared ineffectual in changing national policies.

Since 1977, no industrial country has turned to the IMF for a standby arrangement. However, the developing countries, particularly the oil-importing ones after the two oil shocks and others as well as after the on-set of the debt crisis in the early 1980s, came to depend even more on the IMF for financial support under its newly created facilities (the Oil Facility, the Structural Adjustment Facility, and the Enhanced Structural Adjust-ment Facility) than they had before. For the seven major developed coun-tries, the so-called G-7, their annual economic summits rather than IMF consultation became the forum for discussion and decisionmaking on eco-nomic matters. The IMF was relegated to the role of an informal secretariat for the summits, and it also provided objective analysis and advice and conveyed the interests of its non-G-7 members to the summiteers.

Kahler suggests that the onset of the debt crisis and the subsequent de-cline of private financial flows to developing countries not only reestab-lished IMF's crucial position as a last-resort source of financing for the heavily indebted countries but also of necessity produced closer working relationships among the IMF, private bankers, and central bankers. This meant that a country's signing on to an IMF stabilization program be-came a necessary condition for its being able to conclude a debt-resched-uling and relief agreement with private bankers.

The World Bank initiated its structural adjustment loans (SALs) and sectoral adjustment loans (SECALs) in 1979. Until then (and again in the 1990s) the bank lent mainly to cover the foreign exchange cost of invest-ment projects, mostly in infrastructural sectors. In fact, lending for other sectors, in particular social sectors, was not substantial until the 1970s, perhaps because it was only then that the bank came to recognize poverty alleviation as the goal of all development (in contrast to the ap-proach of some major developing countries such as India, where poverty alleviation had long been the overarching objective of development). SALs and SECALs, in contrast, were in support of policy reform ranging from the reform of trade policy, price controls, and the public sector to policies relating to particular sectors. These reforms were almost always in the self-interest in the *long run* of the borrowing countries but had sig-nificant *short-run* adjustment costs. If private capital was either unavail-able or too costly for financing adjustment that would pay off in the long run, lending by the World Bank in support of reforms could be justified. This assumes that the borrowing countries were convinced that the re-forms were in their own interest.[1] Otherwise, the countries would use borrowed funds for whatever purpose they deemed desirable, imple-menting reforms partially or not at all.

With the IMF having led the World Bank in structural adjustment lend-ing, the earlier distinction between the role of the IMF as a short-term lender for stabilization and the bank as a long-term lender for develop-ment blurred. This also meant greater cooperation, if not coordination, between the two institutions in their lending policies and conditionalities imposed on developing-country borrowers from either. As Kahler (1995: 63) perceptively remarks:

> For nearly two decades, the IMF's lending has been directed exclusively to the developing and ex-socialist economies. In the case of the IMF and World Bank, and to a degree the GATT, the role delegated to the global institutions by the major economic powers is one of wider integration, liberalizing trade regimes, ending price controls, and reforming public sector enterprises may include a certain degree of policy harmonization, but they only set the stage for further economic integration. (Kahler 1995: 63)

The IMF and the World Bank differ from the GATT, and now the WTO, in two crucial respects.[2] First, they both have resources to lend and thus some leverage in imposing conditionality. Of course, conditionality can be imposed only on borrowing countries, which, since the 1970s at least, have not included any developed countries. Second, in their weighted system of voting, with the industrialized countries having the largest weight in their decisionmaking, the influence of developing countries is limited. The WTO has no resources to lend and to be used as leverage to ensure that its policy advice is followed. The GATT tradition has been one of consensus in decisionmaking, although formally, a majority can decide with each member having one vote. Whether the WTO will abandon the consensus tradition and, if so, whether the power disparities will permit the developing countries to combine and use their numerical majority to influence decisions remains to be seen. Even if they do, as the experience of the UN General Assembly has clearly demonstrated, the mere passing of resolutions is likely to be of little consequence.

The WTO is formally required, under its Article III, to cooperate with the IMF and the World Bank. In fact, Article 24 of the charter of the stillborn ITO had spelled out in detail its relationship with the IMF, seeking to coordinate exchange-rate policy under the jurisdiction of the IMF and trade policy matters under the jurisdiction of the ITO. This article became Article XV of the GATT, 1947. The Marrakech ministerial declaration on the relationship of the WTO and the IMF explicitly refers to Article XV as the basis for such a relationship. As noted earlier, the WTO and the IMF signed a cooperation agreement in December 1996, and a similar agreement with the World Bank is in the works.

The economic logic that trade policy measures are inappropriate instruments to address balance-of-payments (BOP) problems arising from inappropriate macroeconomic policies was apparently not accepted either by the architects of the GATT in 1947 or by policymakers in some contemporary industrialized countries (for example, in the United States some advocate the use of trade and industrial policies for addressing persistent current-account deficits). Articles XII and XVIII(B) of the GATT permit the otherwise banned quantitative restrictions (QRs) to be imposed for balance-of-payments reasons. The WTO agreement does not repeal these articles. But there is an understanding that members are committed to announce publicly, as soon as possible, time schedules for the removal of restrictive import measures taken for BOP purposes.[3] Still, as compared to the GATT, in the WTO agreement there is a shift in favor of price-based measures with QRs being exceptional for dealing with BOP problems. It is unclear how the WTO and the IMF will cooperate under Article XV, if read with Articles XII, XVIII:B, and the understanding on BOP provisions! In the past, it was always the IMF that provided BOP data; the World Bank and the IMF together pushed macro, rather than trade, policies for solving BOP problems in their policy dialogue with member countries. The GATT played no role.

Finally, there is the issue of size and resources likely to be available to the WTO secretariat. Both the World Bank and the IMF are large bureaucracies that pride themselves (justifiably or not) on their analytical capability in providing policy advice to their members and rational arguments supporting their conditionalities. Given the history of the GATT, its secretariat was always small. With the establishment of the WTO as a formal organization, a very modest expansion is contemplated. Whereas no one would argue for the WTO secretariat to be expanded into a large, costly, lethargic, and inefficient international bureaucracy (e.g., the UN), there is a legitimate issue concerning whether the proposed expansion is adequate for the secretariat to discharge all the responsibilities assigned to it. The trade policy review mechanism (a very desirable mandate of the WTO that was in fact agreed to in the midterm review of the UR), under which periodic reports on the trade policies of each member country are issued, itself will require significant resources. Besides, several multilateral agreements such as GATS are also under the purview of the secretariat. As noted earlier in Chapter 8, there is a demand to extend the WTO's mandate to include linkage between trade policies and performance with respect to environmental and labor standards. If the secretariat is to do its trade policy reviews in a timely fashion with adequate depth of analysis, if it is to help in many ways any developing country needing assistance in using the WTO's dispute-settlement mechanism, and if it is to monitor compliance with labor and environmental standards, ways have to be found to provide it with adequate resources.

One possibility proposed by some is to scale down, if not abolish, UNCTAD and use the resources thus saved in the WTO. But given the perception (true or false) on the part of the developing countries that UNCTAD is serving their interests, this is politically difficult. Some have already publicly opposed the idea. Alternatively, the cooperation of the WTO with its vastly richer cousins, the IMF and the World Bank, could include the latter assisting the WTO with analytical support. In the absence of some such arrangement, cynics might conclude that the WTO will be deliberately deprived of resources so that it cannot assist developing countries or protect their interests or the environment when pressured by industrialized countries!

Last, the WTO already envisages cross-conditionality—across sectors and across different component agreements—in the sense that a trade sanction in one sector could be imposed on a country for its violation of a provision in the agreement on trade in goods in another sector; more generally, sanction in terms of trade in some goods may be imposed for violation of a provision of the services agreement and so on. It is conceivable that cooperation among the WTO, the IMF, and the World Bank might lead to *cross-institutional conditionality*. Thus industrialized countries, with their greater power in the IMF and the World Bank under the weighted voting system, could leverage that power to "punish" developing countries if they violate the WTO agreement. However, the ministers, in their Marrakech declaration on the contribution of the World Trade Organization to achieving greater coherence in global policymaking, have urged that

> the World Trade Organization should therefore pursue and develop cooperation with the international organizations responsible for monetary and financial matters, while respecting the mandate, the confidentiality requirements and the necessary autonomy in decision-making procedures of each institution, and avoiding the imposition on governments of cross-conditionality or additional conditions. (GATT 1994a: 443)

Although the declaration does not have the force of a formal multilateral agreement, it is to be hoped that it will be observed.

Notes

1. It was noted earlier that Ernest Stern, the former managing director of the World Bank, recognized in the late 1980s the bank's failure to take into account that structural adjustment involves a major redistribution of economic power. Yet a decade later, another study by the World Bank, done by David Dollar and Craig Burnside, in effect stressed the same point. Dollar is quoted to have said that "we got into thinking we could induce countries to reform. But it turns out to be wrong. . . . We have to recognize that positive reform is largely the result of domestic forces." The reporter for the *Financial Times*, Stephanie Flanders, added, "The fact that development programmes have not systematically affected policymaking suggests that official efforts to make support strictly conditional on good policy have not been very successful" (*Financial Times*, April 14, 1997: 18).

2. The debate over the future role of the IMF and the World Bank, triggered by the fiftieth-anniversary observances of the founding of the two, revealed a signif-

icant divergence of views. At one extreme was the Bretton Woods Commission with its nostalgic recommendation for a "return" to the role of a strengthened IMF at the center of international monetary affairs as an agency that ensures the formal coordination of macroeconomic policy among major institutional countries aimed at stabilizing exchange rates. At the other were those who wished to abolish both institutions, one group accusing them of contributing to the perpetuation of poverty and accelerating environmental degradation and the other favoring abolishment for the opposite reason—because they were costly, ineffective, and inferior to private financial markets in financing development. Martin Wolf (*Financial Times*, October 7, 1997: 17) suggests that perhaps the only realistic future is for the two to provide finance and policy advice for the poorest developing countries that lack access to private financial markets and disband when that access is achieved. Although I find Wolf's suggestion sensible, the issue of the future of the two Bretton Woods institutions is too complex to discuss here.

3. Although the retention of these articles in the WTO indicates that there is still no comprehension of the economic logic that the causes and cures of BOP problems have to be sought in macroeconomic policies, the understanding goes part of the way in not allowing countries to continue with their QRs by merely citing BOP problems. The understanding has apparently had some positive results already. According to a report, "India had reached a decision that it would no longer seek exemption from a full liberalisation of its consumer goods sector by claiming balance of payments vulnerability. . . . India would inform the WTO in Geneva next Thursday of its decision to begin talks towards a phased liberalisation of 2500 consumer goods which have remained on a 'negative list' and thus banned from import. . . . The move follows heavy pressure from the US, the European Union and the IMF" (*Financial Times*, May 10–11, 1997: 7).

11 *Summary and Conclusions*

$\mathbf{I}$t was noted in Chapter 2 that more by circumstance than by design, the GATT came to serve as the multilateral framework of international trade relations for nearly half a century. The circumstance was the failure of the United States to ratify the charter of the ITO that emerged from the Havana conference of 1947–1948. Although technically the GATT was not an organization but a multilateral agreement, and even its application was provisional throughout its existence, it nonetheless succeeded in substantially reducing barriers to world trade through eight successive rounds of MTNs held under its auspices. With the agreement reached at the conclusion of the UR, the eighth and the most ambitious of the rounds, a formal international organization, the World Trade Organization (WTO), came into being and subsumed the GATT. As of August 1, 1995, there were 105 members and 46 observers in the WTO and 27 are in the process of negotiating their access.[1] Of the 105 members, 25 are low-income countries and 29 are lower-middle-income countries as per the World Bank classification. Indeed, a substantial majority of the members are developing countries.

Besides bringing the WTO into existence and correcting many of the weaknesses of the GATT, the UR agreement also extended the GATT disciplines to new areas, such as services (under the GATS), and brought trade in agriculture and textiles and apparel back into the GATT disciplines. Agreement was also reached to strengthen the protection of trade-related intellectual property (TRIPs) and liberalize trade-related investment measures (TRIMs). The earlier side treaties and codes, such as antidumping measures and other nontariff barriers, have been brought within the WTO so that their benefits and obligations are available to all its members. The dispute-settlement mechanism of the WTO is stronger than that of the GATT. The available estimates of the growth in merchandise trade and in incomes with the full implementation of the liberalization agreed to in the UR show significant, though modest, gains.

The preceding positive assessment of the achievement of the Uruguay Round is sufficiently widely held to be deemed conventional wisdom. The discussion in the earlier chapters suggests, however, that from the perspective of developing countries, particularly the poorer ones, a much more cautious and nuanced assessment is appropriate. First, any member can withdraw from the WTO after giving six months' prior notice without having to specify any reason whatsoever for its action. Although it would seem unlikely that members who have a significant share in world trade will choose to withdraw, nonetheless, it is disquieting that a proposal has been made for the U.S. Congress to create a panel to review any findings against the United States by the WTO's Dispute Settlement Body (DSB) and mandate that the United States should withdraw from the WTO if the panel finds in three successive occasions that the United States has been unfairly treated by the DSB. Fortunately this proposal has not been enacted. Needless to say, withdrawal by the United States would effectively end the WTO's existence. Thus the DSB could be constrained by the fear that the proposal could be revived and the United States might withdraw if its findings were unacceptable to it. In turn, the anticipation of this constraint on the DSB would deter weaker members of the WTO from bringing any complaint against the United States to the DSB.[2]

Second, from the Havana conference on until and including the prenegotiation phase of the UR, the developing countries did not give up their insistence on special and differential treatment and, in their own assessment, achieved limited success in getting their concerns reflected in the GATT framework. Thus they were ambivalent toward the GATT and, until the Tokyo Round, did not participate actively in it. It is true that the charter of the stillborn ITO had a chapter on economic development that survived as Article XVIII of the GATT; that later a panel of experts appointed by the GATT identified barriers of all kinds in developed countries to imports of products from developing countries and the Committee III was constituted in the GATT to develop a program to reduce these barriers and expand exports of developing countries; and that later still, partly in response to the preparations for UNCTAD I, Part IV on trade and development was added to the GATT. Last, in the Tokyo Round of the MTN, the so-called enabling clause was agreed to; it legitimized the "special, differential and more favorable treatment" of developing countries and the Generalized System of Preferences. In Chapter 3, it was argued that first, these "concessions" to the demands of developing countries achieved a lot in terms of verbiage but precious little by way of precise commitments, and even these were highly qualified. Second, some of these demands themselves were driven by the dogged pursuit of a counterproductive, inward-oriented development strategy of import-substituting industrialization by many developing countries outside of East Asia. The onset of the debt crisis in some inward-oriented countries and the success of East Asia led to a widespread realization among policymakers of the failure of this strategy. As the UR was about to be initiated, many countries had already begun a program of unilateral liberalization of their foreign trade and investment regimes. However, the prenegotiation history of the UR is ample testimony to the reluctance of some major developing countries to enter into another round of MTNs, let alone expand its mandate into new areas.

Had the developing countries not been committed to an inward-oriented development strategy, not insisted on special and nonreciprocal treatment, and participated on equal terms with developed countries, whether they would have achieved greater success in the GATT is an open question. In particular, it is arguable that under those hypothetical circumstances, the developed countries would not have been able to get away for so long with blatantly GATT-inconsistent measures with respect to goods in which developing countries were interested, such as textiles, clothing, and agriculture, while offering a pittance in terms of the GSP, the Lomé convention, and so on and a lot of rhetoric in terms of special and differential treatment. One cannot change the past. Now that the industrialized countries have committed to a ten-year phaseout of MFA and not to institute any other gray-area measures, full and active participation in the WTO of developing countries, now on the side of barrier-free global markets rather than on the side of special treatment, is essential for ensuring that these commitments are kept. Otherwise, with protectionist sentiment rising in industrialized countries, these commitments might have the same fate as earlier agreements about the "stand still and roll back" of GATT-inconsistent measures. Such agreements were viewed by the developing countries as commitments of developed countries; the latter viewed them as no more than requiring "best endeavors" on their part.

Third, the quantitative gains to developing countries from the trade liberalization achieved in the UR are not only modest but also distributed unevenly. Almost all estimates of such gains suggest that sub-Saharan Africa might in fact lose rather than gain.[3] There are two main reasons for this: First, the industrialized countries (and some developing countries) liberalized most of their trade prior to the UR agreement and stood to benefit from the liberalization of other countries under the UR agreement. Second, the dynamic gains to developing countries are likely to be substantial but are difficult to quantify. In the one sector of much interest to developing countries, namely textiles and apparel, the phaseout of the MFA is backloaded—even by the end of the ten-year phaseout period, a significant part of the textile and apparel trade will be subject to barriers. But even if the phaseout is carried out (and there are strong reasons to believe that it will be a politically difficult task in industrialized countries), a substantial part of the gain will accrue to consumers in industrialized countries. This is not to say that developing countries will not gain; indeed they will, but the gain will be much less and will also accrue to the more efficient producers, not necessarily those from poorer countries, among them. The MFA quotas currently protect some of the inefficient ones, and they will be wiped out once the MFA is no longer there. This is certainly not an argument in favor of the MFA but only to make it clear that it was an inefficient contract through which developed countries protected their textile and apparel industries by distributing their quotas widely enough among efficient and inefficient producers and thereby blunting their opposition.

Other than bringing agricultural trade under the discipline of the GATT rules, there is very little liberalization. (And even in agricultural trade coming under GATT rules, there are some exceptions: Whereas the subsidization of exports of manufactures is ruled out, agricultural export subsidies are merely to be reduced but not eliminated, let alone out-lawed.) In the process of converting existing barriers into tariffs and binding their levels, before applying the agreed-upon reductions, many countries, including some developing countries, have set their initial bound level of tariffs very high, even higher than the level of actually ap-plied tariffs in recent years. Although the reduction of export subsidies and domestic support measures (other than the so-called green-box mea-sures, which are assumed not to distort trade) will be of benefit to devel-oping-country exporters, the possible rise in world prices of food grains with the reduction in subsidized exports from developed countries will hurt food-importing developing countries. Of course, not all countries that imported food *prior* to liberalization will necessarily continue to do so *after*—indeed, with the removal of preexisting policy biases against agriculture, some could become exporters. Be that as it may, on balance, agricultural liberalization is likely to be a washout from the perspective of developing countries.

Fourth, the effects of the UR agreement on new issues such as services, TRIMs, and TRIPs, as well as the strengthening of the DSM (the theme of Chapter 6) are of course impossible to quantify. It is likely that gains, if any, may not outweigh costs by a substantial margin for the developing countries. For example, in services, particularly financial services, the do-mestic financial markets are undeveloped and repressed in many devel-oping countries. Their financial sectors have to be reformed, appropriate laws and regulations enacted, and regulatory institutions created where they do not exist to enable domestic providers of financial services to sur-vive the opening up of financial markets to foreign competition. These reforms have to be undertaken whether or not the financial markets are opened. But given the complexity of reforming financial institutions, un-dertaking such reforms while opening them to external competition is a daunting task. It is understandable, therefore, that many developing countries were not very forthcoming in their initial offers and commitments at the time of their accession to the GATS. Indeed, the United States deemed these offers so inadequate as to withdraw its own MFN commitments to the financial services agreement; only the fact that other major countries did not follow the U.S. example saved the agreement from collapsing. This agreement will expire at the end of 1997. Although some developing countries have or will soon attain comparative advantage in financial services and will benefit from their liberalization, many more will benefit if labor-intensive services are liberalized to a considerable extent. GATS does not go far enough in this regard.

Agreement on TRIMs on the whole achieved relatively little and is unlikely to benefit or hurt developing countries to any measurable extent. TRIPs agreement is another matter. At least in the short run, and perhaps even in the longer run, developing countries might lose from stricter intellectual property protection.

On safeguards and dispute settlement, the outlawing, so to speak, of gray-area measures such as voluntary export restraints and import expansions, an eminently desirable objective, seems to have been bought through some weakening of the provisions regarding the use of antidumping and other safeguard measures. In fact, the fear that ADMs might be invoked in the future by developed countries to a greater extent than they have been in the past in order to restrict competition from imports from developing countries (particularly if the phaseout of MFA comes about) is not entirely unfounded (more on this in Chapter 12). Unfortunately, developing countries have also begun to take recourse to antidumping measures to a much greater extent than earlier.

The strengthened DSM is undeniably in the interest of all members of the WTO. The provisions in the UR agreement that make available the services of the WTO secretariat, if needed, to enable the developing countries to avail themselves of the DSM are to be welcomed. Yet realistically speaking, the administrative and information-gathering capabilities of many developing countries are likely to prove inadequate even with the assistance of the WTO secretariat to present a strong case before the DSB. More important, as happened in the past in the GATT, power realities will continue to limit the extent of relief that a weak, developing country can obtain in its dispute against a powerful, industrialized country. However, as noted earlier, the possibility of joint action by a group of aggrieved small countries could have some effect on the powerful. Ultimately, unless the powerful agree to abide by the decisions of the DSB, there is very little the less powerful can do. The United States, after bringing about the strengthening of the DSM in the WTO, as compared to the GATT, chose not to use it in its complaint against Japan on auto parts and unilaterally threatened to impose punitive tariffs on imports of luxury cars from Japan, an action for which there is no legal basis in the WTO.[4] Despite the settlement of this dispute and the optimistic gloss that the director-general of the WTO chose to put on the settlement by calling it a success for WTO's DSM, the facts seem to be otherwise. The WTO was a mere bystander and not a player in any real sense in the settlement of the dispute.

Indeed, in his speech before the Foreign Correspondent's Club in Tokyo on July 31, 1995, Mr. Jeffrey Garten, then the U.S. undersecretary of commerce, had this to say about the use of the WTO in settling future U.S.-Japan trade disputes:

> Many of my Japanese friends—and many Americans and Europeans, too—ask me why we don't use the World Trade Organization to settle all disputes with Japan. They say that a potentially powerful multilateral mechanism now exists in the form of the new World Trade Organization, and that using it would be much less contentious than the bilateral clashes we have had.
>
> This solution has considerable conceptual appeal. . . . We are every bit as committed to the WTO as we have been to its predecessor, the GATT.
>
> But the reality is that the WTO is not yet equipped to handle many of the complex trade issues which are arising in the global arena, and which currently exist between our two countries. Today, for example, we do not believe it can handle many of the complex regulatory issues, nor a variety of anti-competitive or restrictive business practices. Given the very diverse membership, it will take time for the WTO to reach agreement on the rules of behavior in these areas, and to have the competence to deal with them efficiently. One day this will hopefully happen—the sooner, the better, in my view. In the meantime, the United States is—as I mentioned before—committed to opening markets. We'd prefer to do it multilaterally, but if we cannot then we will complement our approach towards the WTO with regional and bilateral approaches.

It is ominous that Mr. Garten chose to declare the WTO to be ill-equipped to deal with complex trade issues rather than call for equipping it soon to deal with them. Whatever benign intent he might have had in mind when he referred to complementing the U.S. approach to the WTO with regional and bilateral approaches to liberalizing market access, it does sound more like a threat that the United States will go regional if the WTO-multilateral approach is too slow or yields too inadequate results from a purely U.S. perspective. This is not at all encouraging from the point of view of weak developing countries, for which the WTO ought to be the guarantor of their interests against threats of the powerful. They would be forced against their interests to seek membership in a regional agreement promoted by the United States were the United States to go aggressively regional.

Fifth, while *multilateral* trade negotiations of the UR for achieving a liberal world trading order were going on, there was an increasing interest in regional and preferential trade arrangements (PTAs), in part triggered by the fear that the UR might fail to be successfully concluded. Yet the interest in PTAs (often misleadingly called free trade agreements, or FTAs) did not die down after the successful completion of the UR. In fact, the membership in NAFTA may soon include Chile as well as Canada, Mexico, and the United States. A decision to achieve free trade and investment in the Western Hemisphere, in the Asia-Pacific region, and in South Asia in the coming two decades or so has also been made. Even a transatlantic free trade area consisting of the European Union and an expanded NAFTA has been proposed. In Chapter 7, it was argued that the claims that such "free trade" agreements are in fact "WTO-plus," in the sense that they include and go beyond the liberalization that could be achieved under the WTO and would push the world closer to global free trade and investment and that the regionalism envisaged in such agreements is not inward-oriented but "open," are overblown. In fact, for most developing countries, unilateral liberalization of trade with all partners on an MFN basis is the best policy.

Sixth, the most serious *external* threat to developing countries in the post–Uruguay Round world trading order is from the attempts to link their market access to performance in nontrade-related areas such as protection of the environment and labor standards. The pernicious notion that a country with lower environmental or labor standards, when it exports its products to another with higher standards, is engaged in eco-dumping and is in unfair competition has gained ground. The UR agreement required the establishment of the Committee on Trade and the Environment in the WTO. This committee has started functioning and has held three meetings since January 1995. The UR agreement almost came apart when, after the Final Act of the UR had been agreed on in December 1993, the United States and France raised the issue of introducing a "social clause" relating to labor standards in the mandate of the WTO. Although this was not agreed to, the demand for a social clause (which has a long history) has not been abandoned. In Chapter 8, it was argued that diversity in labor and environmental standards (at least as far as purely domestic environmental insults are concerned) is legitimate. No country should be coerced to set these standards at levels that are not sustainable given its stage of development. There is also the danger that the movement in developed countries genuinely concerned about environmental degradation and interested in the improvement of labor standards in poor countries will be captured by those who wish to use it for their own crass protectionist purposes. It is clear that if the developed countries are not willing to compensate poor countries for raising their standards beyond what they could sustain on their own but coerce them through denial of access to their own markets, the liberalization of market access in the post-UR world will have no meaning for poor countries.

Seventh, there are serious *domestic* constraints that could get in the way of developing countries reaping the full benefits of the post-UR trading and investment environment. These include a poorly functioning and inadequate infrastructure (transport, power, and telecommunication), rudimentary financial markets, and lack of an appropriate legal framework to support a market economy that is open to the rest of the world. Also, managing a volatile portfolio investment that is attracted to liberalizing developing countries without running into a Mexican-style crisis requires an analytical capacity that few developing countries have. In Chapter 9, these problems were discussed, and it was argued that domestic constraints could reduce but not eliminate the benefits to developing countries from greater integration with the global economy. Thus developing countries should go ahead with such integration.

Eighth, the WTO, a demonstrably much-improved version of the stillborn ITO and a third intended sibling of the Bretton Woods twins, namely the World Bank and the IMF, is at last born. But its birth, five decades late, comes at a time when the roles of the twins themselves are no longer seen as being as vital as they were at the end of World War II. The WTO charter requires it to cooperate with the other two. Such cooperation, if it extends to the sharing by the WTO of the much larger administrative and analytical capabilities of the twins, will be very useful. This is so because whereas the parties to the UR agreement have loaded the WTO secretariat with far more functions (e.g., with respect to the GATS, trade and environment, the trade policy review, and helping developing countries in their dealings with the DSB) than the GATT ever had, they have decided to keep the secretariat small. But if cooperation also means cross-institutional conditionality, in the sense of a country being sanctioned by one institution for its failure to fulfill its obligation to another, it is not necessarily desirable. The reason is that although in the WTO each member has one vote and a majority of the membership is required in its decisionmaking, in the other two, there is a weighted system of voting with the industrialized countries having the largest weight. In such a context, through cross-institutional conditionality, the industrialized countries may be able to leverage their power in the IMF and World Bank to power in the WTO over developing countries.

To conclude, although the UR agreement and the birth of the WTO are indeed major turning points in the history of the world trading and investment system, and the developing countries will almost surely benefit from both, a cautious optimism rather than euphoria is most appropriate in evaluating their potential effects. This is not to deny that the agreement opens up significant opportunities for developing countries. To avail themselves of these opportunities to the fullest extent, decisionmakers have to recognize that a transparent market and an investor-friendly and competitive *domestic* environment is essential. The first steps in establishing such an environment are to liberalize foreign trade, unify the exchange rate, and achieve IMF's Article VIII convertibility status at the earliest and remove restrictions on foreign investment; the next and more difficult steps are domestic reforms in industrial, infrastructural, and financial sectors. But without such reforms, the gains from the initial steps are likely to be modest and might even be short lived.

Notes

1. See Chapter 12 for an updated count.

2. Thus far these fears seem exaggerated: The developing countries have not hesitated to bring complaints against the United States and other industrialized countries before the DSB. See Chapter 12.

3. Amjadi, Reinke, and Yeats (1997) find that inappropriate domestic policies, rather than external barriers, led to the marginalization of sub-Saharan Africa in world trade. If they are right, without a change in these policies, external liberalization following the UR agreement is unlikely to benefit sub-Saharan Africa.

4. Fortunately, the United States decided to use the DSM in its Kodak-Fuji dispute with Japan. See Chapter 12.

12 *Postscript*

Since the previous eleven chapters of this book were written, the membership of the WTO has expanded to 128, and 28 (including China and Russia) negotiated their terms of accession when the first ministerial meeting of the WTO was held at Singapore during December 9–13, 1996. This chapter briefly looks at developments since the end of 1995 on matters relating to international trade and investment from the perspective of developing countries.

In his fourth annual Sylvia Ostry lecture, Mr. Renato Ruggiero, director-general of the WTO, described the achievements of the WTO during its first eighteen months of existence as "a picture of light and shadow, of commitments implemented and others which remain still unfinished business" (WTO 1996b: 4). A good start had been made in the implementation of the UR agreements, but he rightly stressed that there was no room for complacency. The pictures of light include the functioning of WTO's DSM; the conclusion of the telecommunications agreement and the agreement to phase out all tariffs on computers, software, telecom products, and semiconductors; and the decision by ministers, first, not to inscribe the relationship between trade and core labor standards on the WTO agenda, second, not to authorize any new work on the issue in the WTO, and third, to recognize that ILO is the competent body to set and deal with labor standards and with which WTO's secretariat will continue to collaborate. The "shadows" to which Ruggiero referred certainly include the failure to conclude multilateral agreements on financial services, movement of natural persons (i.e., those who provide services), and maritime transport as well as problems with the implementation of parts of the UR agreement, such as the one on textiles and apparel. The disturbing trend toward preferential trade arrangements and the attempts to burden the WTO with matters that are at best tangentially related to trade, such as labor and environmental standards, appear to be stalled, though not dead. Issues such as provisions on investment and competition policy are on the built-in agenda of the WTO. In what follows, I discuss these "lights and shadows" in the context of the Singapore declaration and also touch on the disturbing implications for the global trading system of some recent legislation in the United States.

The Dispute Settlement Understanding and
Safeguard and Antidumping Measures

Renato Ruggiero has claimed with considerable justification that thus far WTO's "best achievement is the dispute settlement body, which is working, and which is really the heart of the multilateral trading system . . . and the system is being used by developed countries, not just developing countries" (interview, *International Herald Tribune*, July 29, 1996: 11). The ministers representing members of the WTO agreed with this assessment when they declared: "We believe the DSU has worked effectively during its first two years. . . . We are confident that longer experience with DSU, including the implementation of panel and appellate recommendations, will further enhance the effectiveness and credibility of the dispute settlement system" (WTO 1997: 8).

Since the start of the WTO, fifty complaints (eighteen initiated by the United States) came before the Dispute Settlement Body (DSB), and ten or so disputes have been settled at the stage of mutual consultation among disputants. Regrettably, the United States, although proclaiming its intention to bring its auto-parts dispute with Japan before WTO's DSB, in fact failed to do so. Fortunately, that dispute was settled by the two parties, and even more significantly, the United States has gone to the DSB with yet another dispute with Japan. This relates to the complaint of Kodak of the United States against Japan that its sales in the Japanese market have been blocked by a series of government measures intended to limit competition with its rival Fuji of Japan. The WTO panel on this dispute is expected to put out its interim report before August and come to a final ruling by October 1997. The EU is supporting the U.S. complaint. Since competition policy and market structure are not yet covered by the WTO, Japan claims that the dispute cannot be the subject of a panel ruling. Also, the United States has decided to accept the ruling on its appeal to the appellate body of the DSM upholding the finding of the panel that investigated Venezuela's complaint about U.S. standards for reformulated and conventional gasoline. According to the *New York Times* (May 9, 1997: A1), in two preliminary reports, WTO panels have upheld the complaint of the United States against the EU—the first with respect to tariff preferences of the EU for banana imports from former European colonies and the second with respect to the ban imposed by the EU on imports of beef and beef products from cattle treated with any of five hormones widely used in the United States but not in Europe. Of twenty-six complaints brought by the United States, four were decided by WTO panels as of the end of April 1997, all in favor of the United States. Of the ten complaints against the United States, three were later suspended or withdrawn; in three the panels ruled against the United States. Unlike the situation that prevailed under the GATT, several developing countries have chosen to take their complaints against some developed countries to the DSB of the WTO. All these augur well for the DSM of the WTO, but there are some disquieting features as well.

From the perspective of developing countries, an important provision in the Dispute Settlement Understanding (DSU) may be its Article 23 on "strengthening the multilateral system." It generally requires members of the WTO to utilize and abide by the rules of WTO's dispute-settlement mechanism (DSM) when any member seeks redress for violation of the WTO rules by another or of nonviolation nullification or impairment of the benefits it is entitled to under the WTO agreement. This was meant to preclude the use of unilateral procedures (e.g., past U.S. actions against several countries, Korea, India, Taiwan, and Thailand, under Section 301 of the U.S. Trade and Competitiveness Act of 1988). India is again on the "watch list" for possible future action under the same section.[1] Thus unilateral measures that are, as Abbott (1995: 32) rightly suggests, "a throwback to power relations" appear to be part of the trade landscape in spite of Article 23.

One of the most serious problems with WTO's unified DS procedure, which is in principle applicable to disputes arising under all the multilateral and plurilateral trading agreements, is that it is subject also to DS rules specific to particular agreements such as the Agreement on Implementation of Article VI of the GATT relating to antidumping measures (ADMs) and countervailing duties. The most important article of this agreement, according to Abbott, is its Article 17.6.[2]

Abbott draws attention to the possibility of an aggressive interpretation of Article 17.6 by WTO DS panels, under which they could make their own determination (rather than requiring the complainant to demonstrate) of whether the impugned national measure was not based on an "objective and unbiased" evaluation of facts and also could assert its own interpretation of the relevant section of the ADM code as the only possible one and deem the national measure as improper if it is different from its own. As Abbott rightly cautions, such an interpretation might lead to a crisis in the WTO legal system. In particular, given the openness and automaticity of the DS system, complaints that challenge politically entrenched programs of powerful states could not be excluded. Such complaints, if sustained by the DSB, might lead these states "to ignore a DS decision or even withdraw from the WTO rather than abandon the programs" (Abbott 1995: 40), thus threatening to undercut the DS system itself.[3]

With many developing countries dramatically lowering their high-tariff and nontariff barriers, it is natural that their domestic import-competing sectors might be tempted to bring complaints of dumping by their foreign competitors. It may be politically difficult to resist pressures for action under the ADM provisions of the WTO agreement. But given the "standard legal review" provision of Article 17.6, it is possible that such AD measures might be found to be WTO-compatible. If this were to occur increasingly, the liberal world trading order of the WTO would be threatened. The developing countries would lose not only by their own use of ADMs but even more if, unfortunately, such use led to a weakening of the WTO. A reconsideration of the ADM code and its relation to WTO's DS system is urgent.

There is another issue with potentially very serious implications on the future of the WTO, namely the Helms-Burton law of the United States, under which non-U.S. companies could be sued by private parties in U.S. courts for "trafficking" in those assets confiscated by the Cuban government from them, and the D'Amato Act, which targets foreign investors in Iran and Libya. In the first of his televised debates with his opponent Robert Dole in the 1996 presidential elections, President Clinton had this to say about the Helms-Burton and the lawsuits that could be filed under it:

> Senator Dole is correct. I did give about six months before effective date of the act before lawsuits can actually be filed, even though they're effective now and can be legally binding, because I want to change Cuba. And the United States needs help from other countries. *Nobody in the world agrees with our policy on Cuba now, but this law can be used as leverage to get other countries to help us to move Cuba to democracy.* (*New York Times*, October 8, 1996: B9, emphasis added)

It should come as no surprise that the foreign ministers of the European Union decided to pursue in the WTO their complaints against Helms-Burton and the anti-Cuba laws and their extraterritorial reach (*Financial Times*, October 3, 1996: 5). In an effort to avoid a major breach with the United States that would threaten the future of the WTO, EU asked the WTO to postpone by a week the naming of a WTO panel on the dispute in an attempt to arrive at a compromise (*New York Times*, February 13, 1997: A1). It failed and a panel was appointed.

Just hours after the appointment of the panel, the United States announced that "it would refuse to take part in the legal proceedings. It declared that the newly-created body [WTO], which was intended to be the arbiter of World Trade Rules 'has no competence to proceed in an issue of American national security'" (*New York Times*, March 21, 1997: A1). John Jackson, in commenting on this claim, said: "The U.S. might be right that this is an issue of national security. But I don't think there is any basis for saying that it can take a walk, without allowing the panel to consider the issue" (*New York Times*, March 21, 1997: A9). If the panel were to accept the U.S. argument, it could open the floodgates for defendants in other cases to use national security as an excuse for breaking the WTO rules (*Financial Times*, October 3, 1996: 3).

After several weeks of intense negotiations, the United States and the EU arrived at a provisional accord under which the U.S. president would undertake to seek an amendment to the Helms-Burton law that would give the president the right to waive the mandated denial of U.S. visas to executives of foreign companies that have violated the law's provisions. In return the EU would agree to the suspension of the WTO panel while retaining the right to reopen its complaints if ever the United States broke its side of the bargain. It is not clear whether the Republican-controlled U.S. Congress will agree to amend the law. Although the compromise "averts the immediate threat that the dispute will escalate further . . . it offers only the basis for a durable settlement and could yet fall apart" (*Financial Times*, April 14, 1997: 4). Although the developing countries are not directly involved in this dispute, if the settlement falls apart and the panel is reactivated, the fallout will surely hurt them regardless of how the panel resolves the dispute.

Service Sectors: Achievements and Failures

Two notable achievements in the service sectors were the conclusion of a telecommunications agreement and the launching of free trade in computer products. The United States had abruptly pulled out of an agreement in April 1996, just a few days before the negotiating deadline, on the grounds that too few nations had made meaningful offers to deregulate and reform. Subsequently many countries improved their earlier offers to accommodate the United States, although it failed to persuade Canada and Japan to give up restrictions that block foreign companies from buying a controlling stake in their domestic telephone carriers. In the agreement that comes into effect on January 1, 1998,

> sixty-nine governments made multilateral commitments in a market that is worth well over half a trillion dollars per year, and these countries account for more than 90 percent of telecoms revenue worldwide. . . . It is difficult to be very precise in these matters, but telecoms liberalization could mean global income gains of some one trillion dollars over the next decade or so. That represents around 4 percent of world GDP at today's prices. (WTO Press Release 67, February 17, 1997)

The biggest impact on consumers is expected to be in the developing world, "where most governments have done little or nothing to reform the creaky state controlled monopolies that provide shabby service at home and charge wildly inflated prices for completing international telephone calls" (*New York Times*, February 16, 1997: A6). However, the legal basis of the GATS agreement provides for filing exemptions from offering the results of the agreement on an MFN basis to all the WTO members. Nine governments including the United States (the only industrialized country) have filed such exemptions.

At the Singapore ministerial meeting, the Declaration on Trade in Information Technology Products was signed by twenty-nine participants accounting for 83 percent of world trade in information technology (IT) products. The declaration provided for the elimination of customs duties and other charges on information technology products through equal annual reductions, to be implemented on an MFN basis applicable to all the WTO members, beginning on July 1, 1997, and concluding in January 2000 (WTO Press Release 69, March 3, 1997). The implementation was contingent on participation (before April 1, 1997) by enough countries to cover approximately 90 percent of world trade in IT products. By March 26, 1997, eleven more had agreed to participate, taking the coverage to 92.5 percent of world trade in IT products, thus meeting the 90 percent criterion for the agreement to be implemented. Two more are expected to announce their participation in the near future. Some seven participants have been granted the flexibility to extend the date for eliminating all tariffs beyond the year 2000 but not beyond 2005.

Success still eludes in coming to a multilateral agreement on the improvement of market access in financial services, the movement of natural persons, and maritime transport. The ministers noted in Singapore that negotiations in these areas have proved difficult and the results were below expectations. However, they expressed their determination "to obtain a progressively higher level of liberalization in services on a mutually advantageous basis with appropriate flexibility for individual developing country members" (WTO 1997: 9).

The negotiations on the liberalization of financial services resumed in Geneva on April 10, 1997, with a deadline of mid-December 1997 to conclude an agreement. As noted in Chapter 6, a proposed earlier agreement had collapsed when the U.S. withdrew at the last minute. A stopgap accord, which expires at the end of 1997, emerged when the EU and other WTO members decided to go ahead without the United States.

> Success this time will require all WTO members to improve substantially on their commitments in that deal, many of which only involved undertakings not to revise existing liberalization. . . . Two factors are inspiring cautious optimism in Geneva. One is the psychological boost from the WTO's agreements this year to free trade in telecommunication services and information technology products—both of which attracted participation by an unexpectedly large number of developing countries. The other positive element is the continuing worldwide trend towards financial market liberalisation. . . . The

question is whether enough countries are willing to accelerate such moves and turn them into formal WTO commitments. . . . Even some which accept the economic case for liberalising are unwilling to yield to international pressure—all the more so when much of it is generated by powerful institutions eager to muscle in on their markets. Furthermore, some developing countries ask why they should go along with a deal that offers them some advantages of interest to their exporters. (de Jonquières 1997: 10)

It is obviously too soon to tell whether the negotiations will succeed.

In the case of services other than maritime transport, the United States did not go along with proposed agreements primarily because of its dissatisfaction with other members' offers. But with respect to maritime transport, the United States did not even make an initial offer of its own, and the negotiations have been postponed to the year 2000.[4]

Implementation of the Uruguay Round Agreement: The Phaseout of the Multifibre Arrangement

The Agreement on Textiles and Clothing (ATC), which is part of the UR agreements, envisaged the integration of the sector into the GATT 1994 through four steps over ten years starting in January 1995. The task of supervising the details of the agreement's implementation is given to the Textiles Monitoring Body (TMB), whose appointed members serve in their personal capacities, not as representatives of their countries, and whose work is overseen by the Goods Council of the WTO.

Two of the cases that came before the TMB were with respect to restrictions imposed by the United States on the imports from India of women's and girls' wool coats and on woven shirts under the safeguards provision. These restrictions went into effect in April 1995. The TMB concluded that in regard to women's and girls' wool coats from India, serious damage had not been demonstrated; in the case of woven shirts and blouses, an actual threat of serious damage from a substantial increase in imports from India had been demonstrated. In October 1995, India asked the TMB to review the two cases again, and in November 1995, the TMB reaffirmed its earlier findings on both cases. On March 27, 1996, India asked the Dispute Settlement Body (DSB) to establish panels to examine its complaints against U.S. restrictions, and the United States did not agree to India's requests for panels. A panel was established at the DSB meeting of April 17, 1996. But the United States removed, with effect from April 24, 1996, its safeguard measures on the imports of women's and girls' wool coats. On April 25, 1996, India asked the DSB to terminate further action on the matter. With respect to safeguard measures imposed by the United States and affecting imports of woven wool shirts and blouses, the panel found on January 6, 1997, that the United States violated the provisions of ATC in imposing them. However, on February 24, 1997, India appealed against certain issues of law and legal interpretations developed by the panel. The appellate body upheld the panel's decisions and interpretations on April 25, 1997.

Hindley (1997a) examines in detail the European Commission's imposition of a provisional antidumping duty (ADD) on imports of unbleached (gray) cotton fabrics originating in the People's Republic of China, Egypt, India, Indonesia, Pakistan, and Turkey. He points out that for an ADD to be consistent with the WTO provisions, it must be shown that imports are dumped, that is, "their price when sold for exports is less than their price in the ordinary course of trade in the home market of the exporter" (p. 3), and that the dumped imports have caused injury to the producers of like products in the importing country. The European Commission added a third condition (not required by the WTO) that the proposed ADD be in its interest. He found that the European Commission's provisional duty determination satisfied none of the three requirements.

Hindley found that the European Commission regulation for the price comparison, to be made whether or not dumping had occurred, differed in critical ways from the corresponding provision in the WTO rules. Second, since the imports on which an ADD was provisionally imposed were subject to quotas under the Multifiber Arrangement (MFA), the quotas were binding. Thus if they were dumped, they could not possibly cause injury to producers of competing products in the EC, since obviously a rise in the price of binding-quota-restricted imports cannot affect the quantity imported and hence the price received by the domestic producers. In a later article, Hindley (1997b) examined the new draft regulation of the European Commission proposing the imposition of *definitive* (rather than *provisional*) ADDs. Although he found that the new regulation apparently corrected the problems raised in the calculation of dumping margins in the earlier regulation imposing a provisional ADD, it still did not recognize that dumped imports cannot cause injury if the volume of imports is restrained by a binding quota. This case illustrates the shape of things to come as the time for the phaseout of the MFA nears.

The developing countries became concerned that U.S. restrictions and EU measures might be the first among many such actions to come. Although such actions have to be terminated by January 1, 2005, in the interim the damage to developing countries could be substantial. A failure to live up to the UR commitments in textiles and apparel would be damaging for yet another reason: The developing countries might then revert to their perception that the WTO, like the GATT, largely subserves the industrialized countries. The director-general of the WTO was clearly aware of the dangers of failing to adhere to the agreed-upon pace of implementation of the phaseout of MFA.[5]

In mid-1996, Pakistan (acting for a group of developing countries, the United States, the EU, and others) presented papers to the WTO Goods Council on the issues relating to the implementation of ATC. "Asian group said the developed importing members were not living up to the liberalizing spirit of the agreement and the interests of the developing countries were not being served. Industrialized members countered that they had fully met the commitment that they had made and argued that some exporting countries retained high import barriers" (WTO 1997: 22–23).

The issues most debated in the papers submitted to the Goods Council related to the pace of the phaseout of MFA, the developing countries complaining that importing countries were using the four-step procedure to postpone until the last day the integration of textiles into the GATT with only one quota being removed in the first step. The developed countries pointed to the agreed-on rise in the growth rates of quotas and predicted that such accelerated growth would make the enlarged quotas nonbinding long before the end of the transition period. The developed countries complained that the high existing tariffs, newly raised applied tariffs, and nontariff barriers in developing countries limited their market access. The responses of the developing countries was that they had complied with the commitment they had made with respect to market access and in any case they opposed linking market access to the quota phaseout.

Other points of debate included safeguard actions in importing countries, actions to prevent circumvention of the ATC, rules of origin, and the transparency of the procedures and impartiality of the TMB. With this background, at Singapore the ministers confirmed their commitment to the full and faithful implementation of ATC. They stressed the importance of bringing trade in textile products under disciplines applicable to trade in all other manufactured goods because of its "systemic significance for the rule-based, non-discriminatory trading system and its contribution to the increase in export earnings of developing countries" (WTO 1997: 22). Whereas there is no reason to doubt the good intentions of the ministers or to be unduly pessimistic about the future, still the political economy of textile protectionism in industrialized countries suggests caution.

Labor and Environmental Standards

In their Singapore declaration, the ministers, although renewing their "commitment to the observance of internationally recognized core labour standards," did not explicitly define them. Instead, they simply asserted, "The International Labour Organization (ILO) is the competent body to set and deal with these standards, and we affirm our support for work in promoting them." They recognized that increased trade and further trade liberalization would foster economic growth and development that in turn would promote core labor standards. They explicitly rejected "the use of labour standards for protectionist purposes, and agreed that the comparative advantage of countries, particularly low-wage developing countries, must in no way be put into question." They noted that in this regard, "the WTO and ILO Secretariats will continue their existing collaboration" (WTO 1997: 7). The chairman of the conference, Yeo Cheow Tang, Singapore's minister of trade and industry, further emphasized what the text of the ministerial declaration did not make explicit: "It does not inscribe the relationship between trade and core and labour standards on the WTO Agenda. . . . There is no authorization in the text for any new work on this issue." Noting the concern expressed by some delegations "that this text may lead the WTO to acquire a competence to undertake further work in the relationship between trade and core labor standards," he assured these delegations that "this text will not permit such a development" (WTO 1997: 13–14).

It is evident that the demand for incorporating a social clause in the WTO was not accepted in Singapore. But this does not mean that the issue is no longer on the international agenda or that trade measures will never be used for enforcing labor standards. First, the director-general of ILO, Michael Hansene, is himself recommending, in a recently published report, that "a global system of social labeling should be introduced to guarantee that internationally traded goods are produced under humane conditions as part of its strategy to link social progress in the workplace more closely to the liberalisation of world trade." Further, Hansene apparently "wants ILO member states to issue a declaration of fundamental rights as a condition for being able to 'share the benefits of globalisation.' This would be binding on all countries belonging to the ILO whether or not they had codified the core labour standards conventions in domestic laws." He also wants the ILO "to introduce regular reports *evaluating* member states' efforts to translate economic development resulting from the *liberalisation of trade* into genuine *social progress*" (*Financial Times*, April 23, 1997: 5, emphasis added). It would be extremely unfortunate if these views represent anything more than the personal opinions of the director-general and in fact are shared by powerful members of the ILO. Even if social progress could be unambiguously defined and measured, since many social, economic, and political factors, and not just trade liberalization, influence it, it would be at best naive and at worst tendentious if the ILO were to issue evaluation reports.

Second, the declaration by the ministers that the ILO is the competent body in matters relating to labor standards does not mean that trade measures, on the use of which the WTO is the competent authority, are ruled out as a means of enforcing labor standards. After all, not only are many nations members of both the ITO and the WTO, but they also constitute a majority in both. Thus if they, as members of ILO, find that its enforcement mechanism is inadequate to ensure compliance of labor standards, they can, in their capacity as WTO members, authorize the use of trade measures.

Third, as more preferential trade agreements with developed and developing countries as members are negotiated, developing countries might have to agree to comply with particular labor and environmental standards in exchange for trade preferences. Otherwise, legislatures in developed countries might not approve such PTAs. Indeed, Mexico had to sign side agreements relating to labor and environmental standards as the price for congressional approval of NAFTA. Legislative leaders in the United States, such as Richard Gephardt of the Democratic Party, have said that in all future negotiations of any PTA of which the United States is to be a member, the observance of labor and environmental standards would have to be part of the PTA agreement itself and not a separate, and in their view weakly enforced, side agreement.

Fourth and finally, unilateral actions have been taken in the past and will continue to be taken in the future by major industrialized countries linking trade or investment with labor standards in particular and human rights more generally. These include WTO-consistent actions such as the withdrawal of preferential access to their markets, access that each developed country can decide on its own to offer to a developing country. The United States has withdrawn such access to Chile in the past. Such unilateral actions also possibly include the WTO-inconsistent laws enacted by individual states in the United States that prohibit purchases by state-owned bodies from companies doing business in Myanmar, formerly Burma (*Financial Times*, April 24, 1997: 8), and the decision of the United States to prohibit future investment by U.S. companies in Myanmar. It is premature, therefore, to celebrate that rationality and the rule of reason have triumphed and that proposals for the use of trade measures to achieve nontrade related objectives are things of the past!

With respect to trade and the environment, the ministerial declaration simply noted the important contribution made by the WTO's Committee on Trade and Environment toward fulfilling its work program and its continuing examination of, "inter alia, the scope of the complementarities between trade liberalization, economic development and environmental protection." Recognizing that "the breadth and complexity of the issues covered by the Committee's work Programme shows that further work needs to be undertaken on all items of its agenda, as contained in its reports," the ministers declared their intention "to build on the work accomplished thus far" and directed the committee "to carry out its work, reporting to the General Council, under its existing terms of reference" (WTO 1997: 9). Since these terms do not call for the examination of the use of trade measures for enforcing environmental standards, the ministerial declaration, by deliberately not expanding the terms to include such an examination, signaled the intention of the ministers to maintain the status quo. However, given that the Committee on Trade and Environment has not been disbanded and is in fact authorized to continue its work, the issue of trade and the environment remains firmly on the agenda of the WTO, thus distinguishing it from the issue of trade and labor standards.

As in the case of labor standards, future unilateral actions (WTO-consistent or otherwise) by industrialized countries to enforce their environmental standards on others through trade action cannot be ruled out. For example, the unilateral action of the United States of banning imports of yellowfin tuna from Mexico on the ground that Mexican fishing methods involved the killing of dolphins, which were protected under the U.S. Mammal Protection Act, was challenged in the GATT by Mexico. Although the GATT panel ruled in favor of Mexico, the two countries settled it bilaterally. But the U.S. ban led to the "so-called Declaration of Panama, a deal between the U.S. and Latin American Nations designed to put safeguards on tuna fishing so that dolphins would not be caught in the nets," and "legislation lifting a U.S. ban on imports of Latin American yellowfin tuna has cleared the fisheries committee of the US House of Representatives but is headed towards an uncertain reception in the full House and Senate" (*Financial Times*, April 18, 1997: 9).

Regional (Preferential) Trading Arrangements

Interest in preferential trading arrangements (PTAs) under which discriminatory trade barriers, based on complex rules of origin that are themselves endogenous responses to protectionist interests, has continued, as noted earlier, even after the conclusion of the UR. Unfortunately, many developing countries seem to be actively engaged in negotiating their membership in one or more such arrangement. However, the reaffirmation of their preference for the multilateral approach by the Asian members of APEC at their Osaka meeting in November 1995 is an encouraging sign against this trend. Also, the extension of NAFTA further into the Americas and its enlargement into a transatlantic free trade area appears to be on hold.

Yet it is an unfortunate fact that the notion that liberalization of trade, even if it is only on a preferential basis among members of a group of countries, is *always* to be applauded is gaining ground.[6] The director-general of the WTO, Renato Ruggiero, seems to agree:

The regional liberalizing impulse is not in itself cause for alarm among the upholders of the multilateral system. Regional initiatives can contribute significantly to the development of multilateral rules and commitments, and in regions such as Sub-Saharan Africa they may be an essential starting-point for integration of least-developed countries into the wider global economy. At the most basic level the real split is between liberalization, at whatever level, and protectionism. Viewed from this perspective regional and multilateral initiatives should be on the same side, mutually supportive and reinforcing. (WTO 1996b: 10)

But he added,

However the sheer size and ambition of recent regional initiatives means we can no longer take this complementarity for granted, if indeed we ever could. We need a clear statement of principles, backed up by firm commitments, to ensure that regional schemes do not act as a centrifugal force, pulling the multilateral system apart.

The answer is to be found, I suggest, in the principle which some of the newer regional groupings have enunciated—*Open Regionalism*. (WTO 1996b: 10)

Ruggiero contrasted two interpretations of open regionalism. The first essentially required that any regional preferential trade arrangement be consistent with Article XXIV of the GATT, 1994, and the understanding on its interpretation incorporated in the UR agreements on trade in goods. In the second, "the gradual elimination of internal barriers to trade within a regional grouping will be implemented at more or less the same rate and on the same timetable as the lowering of barriers towards non-members. This would mean that regional liberalization would in practice as well as in law be generally consistent with the m.f.n. principle" (WTO 1996b: 11). He concluded,

The choice between these alternatives is a critical one; they point to very different outcomes. In the first case, the point at which we would arrive in no more than 20 to 25 years would be a division of the trading world into two or three intercontinental preferential areas, each with its own rules and with free trade inside the area, but with external barriers still existing among the blocs. (WTO 1996b: 11)

He clearly expressed his preference for the second, arguing that it

points towards the gradual *convergence* of regionalism and multilateralism on the basis of shared aims and principles, first and foremost respect of the m.f.n. principle. At the end, we would have one free global market with rules and disciplines internationally agreed and applied to all, with the capacity to invoke the respect of the rights and obligations to which all had freely subscribed. In such a world there could and must be a place for China, Russia and all the other candidates to the WTO. (WTO 1996b: 11)

Notwithstanding the director-general's favored second interpretation, it seems odd to call such liberalization "open regionalism." After all, if such regional liberalization is to be extended *on the same time table* "in practice and in law" to nonmember countries on an MFN basis, then it would be multilateral and not regional. If that is the case, why would any group initiate it on a regional basis in the first place? The concern of the director-general that mere consistency with Article XXIV is not enough to preclude the possibility of a world of warring trade blocs is well taken. In its excellent and well-balanced report on regionalism, the WTO (1995d) documents the dismal failure of the GATT working party mechanism to examine the consistency of any proposed PTA with Article XXIV and make recommendations to the governing council of the GATT. Given this history, steps have to be initiated to strengthen the process of review in the WTO of proposed regional agreements.

A committee on regional trade agreements was established by the General Council of the WTO in February 1996. The committee is to examine twenty-three proposed agreements, presumably for their compatibility with the WTO and the General Agreement on Trade and Services (GATS) and, inter alia, "to consider the systemic implications of such agreements and regional initiatives for the multilateral trading system and the relationship between them, and make appropriate recommendations to the General Council" (WTO 1996d: 10).

The Singapore ministerial declaration (WTO 1997: 7) takes note "that trade relations of the WTO members are being increasingly influenced by regional trade agreements, which have expanded vastly in number, scope and coverage" and views the trend somewhat benignly by saying that "such initiatives can promote further liberalization, and may assist least-developed, developing and transition economies in integrating into the international trading system." While reaffirming "the primacy of the multilateral trading system, which includes a framework for the development of regional trade arrangement" and renewing their commitment "to ensure that regional trade agreements are complementary to it and consistent with its rules," the ministers welcomed the establishment of the WTO's Committee on Regional Trade Agreements and endorsed its work. It is to be seen whether the committee will have greater success than the working parties of the GATT had in the past in examining the compatibility of regional agreements with Article XXIV and whether it will resist the temptation to put political compulsions above the need to assess the seriousness of the threat posed by such agreements to the principle of nondiscrimination, which is the foundation of the WTO. In Srinivasan (1997), I have suggested that the committee might consider replacing Article XXIV with a better alternative that is precise, transparent, and predictable in its application.

An attractive alternative is one that retains the notification requirements of Article XXIV and lays down a precise time limit (say five years)
within which *any and all* preferences (tariff and nontariff) that are included in any existing or proposed PTAs are required to be extended to
all members of the WTO on an MFN basis; also, in the case of customs
unions, if the common external tariff structure results in an increase in a
tariff relative to what prevailed in any country prior to its becoming a
member, such increases are to be rescinded within the same period; finally, in the case of FTAs, *any increase* in the applied external tariffs of a
member following its formation, even if it is within its previously bound
levels, are to be rescinded within the same period. Any disputes relating
to the observance of these conditions would be resolved using the DS
mechanism of the WTO. This alternative restores nondiscrimination
within a set time limit and avoids having to examine whether PTAs sat-
isfy specified conditions to be given a permanent waiver from the MFN
principle. But given that, in effect, it proscribes PTAs, including existing
ones such as the EU and NAFTA, except for a brief period of time, it may
not attract political support.

While awaiting the WTO committee's report, the developing countries
would do well to pause before rushing into any regional PTAs. Caution is
warranted also for the reason that some evidence is now emerging that
the two regional agreements in the Western Hemisphere, namely NAFTA
and MERCOSUR, may be diverting the trade of nonmembers to members. "NAFTA's devastating effect on the Caribbean was widely forecast
before the treaty's passage in 1993, and Washington suggested it would
cushion the blow by extending similar preferences to the island nation.
However, the Clinton Administration's proposals to give the Caribbean
'NAFTA parity' have twice floundered in Congress" (*New York Times*,
January 30, 1997: A1). But in the meantime, "from the apparel plants of
Jamaica to the sugarcane fields of Trinidad, NAFTA has resulted in the
loss of jobs, markets and income for the vulnerable nations of the region.
The capital and investment projects that are vitally needed for future
growth, officials say, are flowing out of the Caribbean basin into Mexico"
(*New York Times*, January 30, 1997: A1). In a study that created contro-
versy and even demands for its suppression, Alexander Yeats (1997) of
the World Bank concludes from his analysis of MERCOSUR that "the
findings of this study appear to constitute convincing evidence that regional preferences can affect trading patterns strongly and in ways that
can be detrimental to both member and non-member countries" (p. 30).
Understandably, he cautions that his study does not comment on "many
other possible effects of RTA's such as benefits from political cooperation,
enhancing the credibility of reform strategies, or dynamic gains from
trade" (p. iii).

Trade and Investment

With respect to investment, the question is whether the members of the WTO should create a comprehensive multilateral discipline to govern foreign investment, particularly foreign direct investment (FDI).[7] To assist the members in analyzing the issues involved, the WTO secretariat recently published a report on trade and FDI (WTO 1996e). The report notes the growing importance of FDI as well as its geographical concentration, both in terms of countries of origin and of destination:

- During 1986–89 and again in 1995, outflows of FDI grew much more rapidly than world trade. Over the period 1973–95, the estimated value of annual FDI outflows multiplied twelve times (from $25 billion to $315 billion), while the value of merchandise exports multiplied eight and a half times (from $575 billion to $4,900 billion).
- Sales of foreign affiliates of multinational corporations (MNCs) are estimated to exceed the value of world trade in goods and services (the latter was $6,100 billion in 1995).
- Intra-firm trade among MNCs is estimated to account for about one-third of world trade, and MNC exports to all other firms for another third, with the remaining one-third accounted for by trade among national (non-MNC) firms.
- Developed countries account for most of the worldwide FDI outflows and inflows, but developing countries are becoming more important as host and home countries.
- The share of the non-OECD countries in worldwide FDI inflows, which decreased in the 1980s, increased from nearly 20 to about 35 per cent between 1990 and 1995. However, these flows were highly concentrated, with 10 countries receiving nearly 80 per cent of the total ($78 billion out of $102 billion).
- Nearly one-third of the 10 leading host economies for FDI during 1985–95 are developing economies. China is in fourth place, with Mexico, Singapore, Malaysia, Argentina, Brazil and Hong Kong also on the list.
- Non-OECD countries accounted for 15 per cent of worldwide outflows of FDI in 1995, compared with only 5 per cent in the period 1983–87. (WTO 1996e: 52–53)

The fact that there are economic and institutional linkages between trade and investment is well recognized. It is also well known that not all forms of FDI (e.g., investment that is in response to high barriers to imports) are necessarily desirable from the perspective of the welfare of citizens of host countries. Restrictive practices by transnational corporations could hurt as well. Of course, beneficial effects through technology transfer and the expansion of export markets are documented as well. The UR agreement on TRIMs and GATS both represented multilateral approaches to some aspects of investment. It is fair to say, however, that the perceived need for a framework to protect and promote foreign investment has resulted in a proliferation of bilateral investment treaties (including some among developing countries), regional initiatives as part of preferential trading agreements (e.g., APEC, ASEAN, EU, MERCOSUR, NAFTA), and a few plurilateral agreements (e.g., the European Energy Charter Treaty). Although bringing order, through a comprehensive multilateral treaty, to the possible chaos created by this proliferation is certainly desirable, it is much too soon to initiate negotiations whether or not they are undertaken under the auspices of the WTO.

The reasons for caution are several. I will mention just two. First, in contrast to trade in goods and services, the issue of national sovereignty is involved in a much more direct way in the case of foreign investment. Most developing countries became sovereign only after the end of World War II. It is understandable that they are still very sensitive to agreeing to negotiations that might call for them to compromise their sovereignty. However, sensitivity to threats against sovereignty is not unique to developing countries. After all, many in the U.S. Congress consider the WTO's DSM as posing a threat to U.S. sovereignty. More important, the failure of the United States to sign or ratify several ILO conventions has been attributed by Charnovitz (1995: 178) to the fear that ratifying a convention could lead to its enforcement by domestic courts, thus superseding any federal or state laws that might be in conflict with the convention. Further, many Americans apparently are reluctant to have U.S. policy reviewed by any international organization.

Second, most of the economic and policy analyses relating to transnational companies and FDI have been done from the perspective of developed countries. Proposed investment codes, formulated by the OECD, draw on this work. It is natural that issues such as the right of establishment, transparency, national treatment, and so on are viewed from the perspective of easing the entry of transnationals. Still, developing countries are rightly concerned about restrictive practices and potential collusive behavior by transnationals and the competition among developing countries to attract them through fiscal incentives. Any proposed code has to address the possibly ruinous, race-to-the-bottom competition through subsidies for it to be attractive to developing countries. After all, with respect to goods, trade subsidies (except in agriculture) are against WTO rules. This is not to say, of course, that a race to the bottom is inevitable or that transnationals will necessarily engage in restrictive practices. Yet in the absence of a thorough study of various concerns of developing countries, their rushing into negotiations with codes only from the organizations of developed countries (e.g., OECD) as negotiating texts would not be advisable. Clearly, such a study could be undertaken by a

body of experts under the aegis of the Centre for Transnational Corporations in UNCTAD or some other such organization.

I would also note that although active efforts to promote the free flow
of capital across national borders through an investment code are being
made, there is a curious asymmetry when it comes to labor flows. In fact,
there is a deafening silence on the part of rich members of the WTO when
it comes to the migration of labor across national borders from poor to
rich countries. Clearly, as noted earlier, if the concern about low labor
standards in poor countries arises from altruism on the part of citizens of
rich countries, such citizens could pressure their own governments to lift
any restrictions on the immigration of workers from countries with low
labor standards. This would be a *direct and a far more effective means* of ex-
pressing their concerns than relying on the indirect means through linking trade and labor standards in the form of a social clause in the mandate of the WTO.

The Singapore ministerial declaration is rightly cautious and endorses
a study of the issues involved. It says,

> Having regard to the existing WTO provisions on matters related to invest-
> ment and competition policy and the built-in agenda in these areas, including
> under the TRIMs Agreement, and on the understanding that the work under-
> taken shall not prejudge whether negotiations will be initiated in the future,
> we also agree to: establish a working group to examine the relationship be-
> tween trade and investment; and establish a working group to study issues
> raised by Members relating to the interaction between trade and competition
> policy, including anti-competitive practices, in order to identify any areas that
> may merit further consideration in the WTO framework. (WTO 1997: 10)

Another Round of MTN?

The ministers agreed at their Singapore meeting to hold their next conference in 1998 in Geneva. Whereas it is true that ministerial meetings offer
opportunities to enter into or take steps toward multilateral agreements
in particular products and sectors (for example, following the Singapore
declaration on trade in information technology products, an agreement
was reached), it would seem that the time is ripe for initiating another
round of MTNs to complete the unfinished tasks of the UR. First, although MTNs are exceedingly complex compared with negotiations with
respect to particular sectors or products, they offer opportunities for bar-
gains across sectors while protecting weaker countries from being ex-
ploited sector by sector or product by product. Second, if unchecked, the
trend toward regional and preferential trade agreements with complex
rules of origin and differing approaches to competition policies, investment, the environment, and labor standards could undermine the

progress toward a liberal system of international exchange. A new round of MTNs is needed to address these issues. Third, as noted in the previous chapters, agricultural trade is still far from being integrated into the WTO, and a new round could at last tackle this task. Fourth, differences with respect to MFN and NT between the GATT 1994, the GATS, and other components of the UR agreement need to be resolved. Last but not least, some of the agreements providing preferential access of developing countries to markets of developed countries (e.g., the Lomé convention) are to expire soon. The start of a new round will enable the developing countries to reflect on whether they should seek the renewal of such arrangements or at last become equal members of the world trading and financial system. In the previous chapters, I have argued that the latter course of action is in the best interests of the developing countries.

Notes

I have drawn from Srinivasan (1996b) in writing this chapter.

1. Section 301 provides for the use of WTO's DSM and authorizes action if it fails to address U.S. concerns.
2. This article "sets forth a unique 'standard of review' for DS panels reviewing national ADMs, as demanded by the United States in November 1993.

"Under art. 17.6, a DS panel may review the facts determined by national ADM authorities, but its review must be limited to whether the authorities properly established those facts (an ambiguous phrase not otherwise defined) and whether their evaluation of the facts was 'unbiased and objective.' If these standards are met, the panel may not make different factual findings. The panel is also authorized to interpret the applicable provisions of the ADM Code. If the national authorities adopt a 'permissible' interpretation of the Code, however, the panel must uphold it, even if the panel concludes that a different interpretation is preferable. . . .

Unlike the rest of the Code, which establishes objective rules to govern ADMs, the standard of review attempts to carve out an area of national discretion. Unlike the Understanding, which creates a powerful DS procedure, the standard of review attempts to limit the authority of WTO DS institutions. The standard of review is based on a faulty analogy, to judicial review of administrative decisions within a national legal system. It undercuts an important purpose of a global agreement by opening the door to inconsistent national practices. Finally, it sets a dangerous precedent by introducing a device that allows states to agree to strong rules in principle while retaining the ability to dilute them in practice (Abbott 1995: 38–39).

3. That this concern is a very serious one is illustrated by the fact that former senator Robert Dole had proposed "a WTO Dispute Settlement Review Commission made up of federal judges. The Commission would review final WTO decisions adverse to the U.S. to determine whether the panel or the Appellate Body

acted improperly. If the Commission made three affirmative decisions in a five-year period, any member of Congress could initiate an expedited legislative procedure potentially leading to withdrawal from the WTO. Failure to apply Art. 17.6 is an explicit basis for an affirmative decision. The WTO DS institutions will almost certainly try to avoid kicking off the WTO era with such a clear challenge to its most powerful member" (Abbott 1995: 40). As yet, the Congress has not taken any action on Senator Dole's proposal.

4. It is no surprise that domestic political considerations, particularly with a forthcoming presidential election in 1996, had a lot to do with this outcome. According to David Sanger (*New York Times*, October 3, 1996: 1), "it took six years and endless arm-twisting for American trade negotiators to persuade Japan, Korea and nearly every European nation to end one of the biggest forms of corporate welfare in the world: billions of dollars in government subsidies for shipbuilders. The subsidies, American shipbuilders said, were making it impossible for them to compete and could cost thousands of jobs in shipyards from Maine to California. But nearly two years after the deal was struck, and just as most subsidies were supposed to be cut off, the entire deal unraveled when Democrats and Republicans in Congress, only weeks from the election, realized that the United States would also have to cut off its subsidies for American shipbuilders."

5. In one of his talks, Ruggiero said: "It is not possible to talk seriously about furthering a relationship of mutual confidence with developing countries unless the industrial countries are ready to act courageously in this sector. There is considerable anxiety among textile exporting developing countries—who also include some of the least-developed—that the major importers are not always living up to the spirit of the Uruguay Round agreement, whatever their observance of its letter. The developing countries are not seeking to rewrite the rules, but they are concerned to have a second integration phase that is more commercially meaningful, and they are anxious about what the end-loading of the commitments will mean in terms of the pressures importing countries face when they finally come to be implemented" (WTO 1996c: 4).

6. Lawrence Summers, the U.S. undersecretary of the treasury, argued in 1991: "Economists should maintain a strong, but rebuttable, presumption in favor of all lateral reductions in trade barriers, whether they be multi-, uni-, bi-, tri-, plurilateral. Global liberalization may be best, but regional liberalization is very likely to be good" (Bhagwati and Krueger, 1995: vii).

7. I thank Jagdish Bhagwati for helpful comments on this issue.

Bibliography

Abbott, Kenneth. 1995. "Trade Remedies and Legal Remedies: Anti-Dumping, Safeguards, and Dispute Settlement After the Uruguay Round." Unpublished manuscript.

Ackerman, B. 1994. "Political Liberalisms." *Journal of Philosophy* 91(7), pp. 364–386.

_____. 1971. *Social Justice in the Liberal State*. Cambridge, Mass.: Harvard University Press.

Alam, Asad. 1992. "Labor Standards and Comparative Advantage." Unpublished doctoral dissertation, Columbia University.

Amjadi, Azita, Ulrich Reinke, and Alexander Yeats. 1997. "Did External Barriers Cause the Marginalization of Sub-Saharan Africa in World Trade?" Discussion paper 348, World Bank, Washington, D.C.

Anderson, Kym, and Richard Blackhurst, eds. 1993. *Regional Integration and the Global Trading System*. New York: Harvester/Wheatsheaf.

Baldwin, Richard. 1993. "A Domino Theory of Regionalism." Discussion paper 857, Centre for Economic Policy Research, London.

Barfield, C. 1995. "Regionalism and U.S. Trade Policy." Paper presented at the Conference on Capital Flows and Regionalism organized by the International Economic Research Center, University of Maryland, and the American Enterprise Institute, June 12–13, 1995; revised version reprinted in Jagdish Bhagwati and Arvind Panagariya, eds., *The Economics of Preferential Trade Agreements*. Washington, D.C.: AEI Press.

Bhagwati, Jagdish. 1995. "U.S. Trade Policy: The Infatuation with Free Trade Areas." In J. Bhagwati and A. Krueger, *The Dangerous Drift to Preferential Trade Agreements*. Washington, D.C.: AEI Press, pp. 1–18.

_____. 1994. "Policy Perspectives and Future Directions: A View from Academia." In U.S. Department of Labor, *International Labor Standards and Global Economic Integration: Proceedings of a Symposium*. Washington, D.C.: Bureau of International Labor Affairs, U. S. Department of Labor, pp. 57–62.

_____. 1993. "Regionalism and Multilateralism: An Overview." In Jaime De Melo and Arvind Panagariya, eds., *New Dimensions in Regional Integration*. Cambridge: Cambridge University Press, pp. 22–51.

Bhagwhati, J. and A. Krueger, *The Dangerous Drift to Preferential Trade Agreements*, Washington D.C.: AEI Press.

Bhagwati, Jagdish, and Arvind Panagariya. 1996. "Preferential Trading Areas and Multilateralism: Strangers, Friends or Foes?" In Jagdish Bhagwati and Arvind

Panagariya, eds., *The Economics of Preferential Trade Agreements*. Washington, D.C.: AEI Press, pp. 1–78.

Bhagwati, Jagdish, and T. N. Srinivasan. 1996. "Trade and the Environment: Does Environmental Diversity Detract from the Case for Free Trade?" In Jagdish Bhagwati and Robert Hudec, eds., *Fair Trade and Harmonization: Prerequisites for Free Trade?* Vol. 1, *Economic Analysis.* Cambridge, Mass.: MIT Press, pp. 159–224.

Bliss, Christopher. 1994. *Economic Theory and Policy for Trading Blocks.* New York: Manchester University Press.

Braga, Carlos A. Primo. 1996. "Trade-Related Intellectual Property Issues: The Uruguay Round Agreement and Its Economic Implications." In Will Martin and L. Alan Winters, eds., *The Uruguay Round and the Developing Countries.* Cambridge: Cambridge University Press, pp. 341–379.

Brandão, Antonio, and Will Martin. 1993. "Implications of Agricultural Trade Liberalization for the Developing Countries." *Agricultural Economics* 8, pp. 313–343.

Brown, Drusilla, Alan Deardorff, and Robert Stern. 1996. "International Labor Standards and Trade: A Theoretical Analysis." In Jagdish Bhagwati and Robert Hudec, eds., *Fair Trade and Harmonization: Prerequisites for Free Trade?* Vol. 1, *Economic Analysis.* Cambridge, Mass.: MIT Press, pp. 227–280.

Brown, Drusilla, Alan Deardorff, Alan Fox, and Robert Stern. 1996. "The Liberalization of Services Trade: Potential Impacts in the Aftermath of the Uruguay Round." In Will Martin and L. Alan Winters, eds., *The Uruguay Round and the Developing Countries.* Cambridge: Cambridge University Press, pp. 292–315.

Charnovitz, Steve. 1995. "Promoting Higher Labor Standards." *Washington Quarterly* 18(3), pp. 167–190.

_____. 1994. "Promoting World Labor Rules." *Journal of Commerce*, April 19.

_____. 1987. "The Influence of International Labor Standards on the World Trading Regime: A Historical Review." *International Labor Review* 126, 565–584.

Cline, William. 1990. *The Future of World Trade in Textiles and Apparel.* Washington, D.C.: Institute for International Economics.

Cooper, Richard. 1995. "The Rise of the Region-State." Review of *The End of the Nation State* by Kenichi Ohmae, *New York Times Book Review*, July 16, 1995, p. 22.

Council of Economic Advisors. 1995. *Economic Report of the President 1995.* Washington, D.C.: Council of Economic Advisors.

Dam, Kenneth. 1970. *The GATT: Law and International Economic Organization.* Chicago: University of Chicago Press.

de Jonquières, G. 1997. "Vision of a Global Market." *Financial Times*, April 10, 1997, p. 10.

De Melo, Jaime, and Arvind Panagariya. 1993. "Introduction." In Jaime De Melo and Arvind Panagariya, eds., *New Dimensions in Regional Integration.* Cambridge: Cambridge University Press, pp. 3–21.

De Melo, Jaime, and David Tarr. 1990. "Welfare Costs of U.S. Quotas in Textiles, Steel, and Autos." Discussion paper 401, Centre for Economic Policy Research, London.

Edwards, Sebastian. 1995. "Comments." In Stephan Haggard, *Developing Nations and the Politics of Global Integration.* Washington, D.C.: Brookings Institution, pp. 123–140.

Finger, J. Michael. 1996. "Legalized Backsliding: Safeguarding Provisions in the GATT." In Will Martin and L. Alan Winters, eds., *The Uruguay Round and the Developing Countries*. Cambridge: Cambridge University Press, pp. 316–340.

François, Joseph, Bradley McDonald, and Hakan Nordström. 1996. "The Uruguay Round: A Numerically Based Qualitative Assessment." In Will Martin and L. Alan Winters, eds., *The Uruguay Round and the Developing Countries*. Cambridge: Cambridge University Press, pp. 253–291.

GATT. 1994a. *The Results of the Uruguay Round of Multilateral Trade Negotiations: The Legal Texts*. Geneva: GATT Secretariat.

GATT. 1994b. "Market Access for Goods and Services: Overview of the Results." In GATT, *The Results of the Uruguay Round of Multilateral Trade Negotiations*. Geneva: GATT Secretariat.

GATT. 1994c. "News of the Uruguay Round of Multilateral Trade Negotiations: The Final Act, Press Summary." *Uruguay Round Newsletter* no. 084 (Geneva: Information and Media Relations Division, GATT).

GATT. 1979. *Report on Multilateral Trade Negotiations*. Geneva: GATT Secretariat.

Goldin, Ian, and O. Knudsen, eds. 1990. *Agricultural Trade Liberalization: Implications for the Developing Countries*. Paris and Washington, D.C.: OECD and World Bank.

Goldin, Ian, and Dominique van der Mensbrugghe. 1996. "Assessing Agricultural Tariffication Under the Uruguay Round." In Will Martin and L. Alan Winters, eds., *The Uruguay Round and the Developing Countries*. Cambridge: Cambridge University Press, pp. 156–182.

Goto, Junichi. 1989. "The Multifibre Arrangement and Its Effects on Developing Countries." *World Bank Research Observer* 5(2), pp. 203–227.

Haggard, Stephan. 1995. *Developing Nations and the Politics of Global Integration*. Washington, D.C.: Brookings Institution.

Harrison, Glenn, Thomas Rutherford, and David G. Tarr. 1996. "Quantifying the Uruguay Round." In Will Martin and L. Alan Winters, eds., *The Uruguay Round and the Developing Countries*. Cambridge: Cambridge University Press, pp. 216–252.

Hathaway, Dale. 1987. *Agriculture and the GATT: Rewriting the Rules*. Washington, D.C.: Institute for International Economics.

Hathaway, Dale, and Merlinda Ingco. 1996. "Agricultural Liberalization and the Uruguay Round." In Will Martin and L. Alan Winters, eds., *The Uruguay Round and the Developing Countries*. Cambridge: Cambridge University Press, pp. 30–58.

Hertel, Thomas, Will Martin, Koji Yanagishima, and Betina Dimaranan. 1996. "Liberalizing Manufactures Trade in a Changing World Economy." In Will Martin and L. Alan Winters, eds., *The Uruguay Round and the Developing Countries*. Cambridge: Cambridge University Press, pp. 183–215.

Hindley, Brian. 1997a. "EC Anti-Dumping: Has the Problem Gone Away?" Unpublished manuscript, Centre for European Policy Studies.

_____. 1997b. "Anti-Dumping in Grey Cotton Fabric: Have the Problems Gone Away?" Working paper, London School of Economics.

Hoekman, Bernard. 1996. "Assessing the General Agreement on Trade in Services." In Will Martin and L. Alan Winters, eds., *The Uruguay Round and the Developing Countries*. Cambridge: Cambridge University Press, pp. 88–124.

_____. 1995. *Trade Laws and Institutions*. Washington, D.C.: World Bank.

Hudec, Robert. 1987. *Developing Countries in the GATT Legal System*. London: Trade Policy Research Centre.

Hufbauer, Gary, Jeffrey Schott, and Kimberly Elliott. 1990a. *Economic Sanctions Reconsidered: History and Current Policy*. Washington, D.C.: Institute for International Economics.

_____. 1990b. *Economic Sanctions Reconsidered: Supplemental Case Histories*. Washington, D.C.: Institute for International Economics.

Hufbauer, Gary, and Kimberly Elliott. 1994. *Measuring the Costs of Protection in the United States*. Washington, D.C.: Institute for International Economics.

Hufbauer, Gary, and Jeffrey Schott. 1994. *Western Hemisphere Economic Integration*. Washington, D.C.: Institute for International Economics.

Jackson, John. 1990. *Restructuring the GATT System*. London: Pinter.

_____. 1989. *The World Trading System*. Cambridge, Mass.: MIT Press.

Johnson, Harry. 1958. "The Gains from Freer Trade with Europe: An Estimate." *Manchester School* 26(September), pp. 247–255.

Kaempfer, William H., Anton D. Lowenberg, H. Naci Mocan, and Kudred Topyan. 1992. "International Sanctions and Anti-apartheid Policies in South Africa: An Empirical Investigation." Working paper, University of Colorado, Boulder.

Kahler, Miles. 1995. *International Institutions and the Political Economy of Integration*. Washington, D.C.: Brookings Institution.

Kemp, M., and H. Wan, Jr. 1976. "An Elementary Proposition Concerning the Formation of Trade Unions." *Journal of International Economics* 6(1), pp. 95–98.

Krueger, Anne. 1995a. "NAFTA: Strengthening or Weakening the International Trading System." In J. Bhagwati and A. Krueger, *The Dangerous Drift to Preferential Trade Arrangements*. Washington, D.C.: AEI Press, pp. 19–33.

_____. 1995b. *Trade Policies and Developing Nations*. Washington, D.C.: Brookings Institution.

Krueger, Anne, M. Schiff, and A. Valdes. 1988. "Agricultural Incentives in Developing Countries: Measuring the Effect of Sectoral and Economy-wide Policies." *World Bank Economic Review* 2(3), pp. 255–272.

Lawrence, Robert. 1994. *Regionalism, Multilateralism and Deeper Integration*. Washington, D.C.: Brookings Institution.

Levy, Philip. 1995. "Free Trade Agreements and Inter-Bloc Tariffs." Unpublished manuscript, Economic Growth Center, Yale University.

Low, Patrick. 1995. "Impact of the Uruguay Round on Asia: Trade in Services and Trade-Related Investment Measures." Unpublished manuscript.

_____. 1993. *Trading Free*. New York: Twentieth Century Fund.

Low, Patrick, and Arvind Subramanian. 1996. "Beyond TRIMS: A Case for Multilateral Action on Investment Rules and Competition Policy?" In Will Martin and L. Alan Winters, eds., *The Uruguay Round and the Developing Countries*. Cambridge: Cambridge University Press, pp. 380–408.

Low, Patrick, and Alexander Yeats. 1994. "Nontariff Measures and Developing Countries: Has the Uruguay Round Leveled the Playing Field?" Policy research working paper 1353, World Bank, Washington, D.C.

Mahalanobis, P. C. 1969. "'The Asian Drama': An Indian View." *Sankhyā: The Indian Journal of Statistics*, Series B, vol. 31, pts. 3, 4.

Maier, Heribert. 1994. "The Perspective of the International Labor Organization." In U.S. Department of Labor, *International Labor Standards and Global Economic Integration: Proceedings of a Symposium.* Washington, D.C.: Bureau of International Labor Affairs, U. S. Department of Labor, pp. 9–14.

Martin, Will, and L. Alan Winters. 1996. "The Uruguay Round: A Milestone for the Developing Countries." In Will Martin and L. Alan Winters, eds., *The Uruguay Round and the Developing Countries.* Cambridge: Cambridge University Press, pp. 1–29.

Ohmae, Kenichi. 1995. *The End of the Nation State.* New York: Free Press.

Panagariya, Arvind. 1994. "East Asia and the New Regionalism in World Trade." *World Economy* 17(6), pp. 817–839.

Parikh, Kirit, G. Fischer, K. Frohberg, and O. Gulbrandsen. 1988. *Towards Free Trade in Agriculture.* Norwell, Mass.: Kluwer Academic.

Rawls, John. 1993a. *Political Liberalism.* New York: Columbia University Press.

———. 1993b. "Law of Peoples." In S. Shuto and S. Hurley, eds., *On Human Rights.* New York: Basic Books, pp. 41–82.

Reich, Robert. 1994. "Keynote Address." In U.S. Department of Labor, *International Labor Standards and Global Economic Integration: Proceedings of a Symposium.* Washington, D.C.: Bureau of International Labor Affairs, U.S. Department of Labor, pp. 1–6.

Rodrik, Dani. 1995. "Comments." In Anne Krueger, *Trade Policies and Developing Nations.* Washington, D.C.: Brookings Institution, pp. 101–111.

Scherer, F. M. 1994. *Competition Policies for an Integrated World Economy.* Washington, D.C.: Brookings Institution.

Schott, Jeffrey. 1994. *The Uruguay Round.* Washington, D.C.: Institute for International Economics.

Srinivasan, T. N. 1997. "Regionalism and the World Trade Organization: Is Nondiscrimination Passé?" In Anne O. Krueger, ed., *The World Trade Organization as an International Institution.* The University of Chicago Press, forthcoming.

———. 1996a. "The Uruguay Round and the Asian Developing Economies." In M. G. Quibria and J. Malcolm Dowling, eds., *Current Issues in Economic Development: An Asian Perspective.* Hong Kong: Oxford University Press, pp. 229–274.

———. 1996b. "Post-Uruguay Round Issues for Asian Developing Countries." *Asian Development Review* 14(1), pp. 1–43.

———. 1996c. "International Trade and Labor Standards from an Economic Perspective." In Pitou van Dijck and Gerrit Faber, eds., *Challenges to the New World Trade Organization.* Amsterdam: Kluwer Law International, pp. 219–243.

Srinivasan, T. N., and Gustavo Canonero. 1995. "Preferential Trading Arrangements in South Asia: Theory, Empirics and Policy." Unpublished manuscript, Yale University.

Subramanian, Arvind. 1995. "Trade-Related Intellectual Property Rights and Asian Developing Countries: An Analytical View." Unpublished manuscript.

Thomas, Vinod, Ajay Chhibber, Mansoor Dailami, and Jaime De Melo. 1991. *Restructuring Economies in Distress.* Oxford: Oxford University Press.

Thorstensen, Vera, and Felix Peña. 1997. "Access to the European Union Market: The View from Latin America." Paper presented at the Fourth Annual Workshop on Multi-lateralism and Regionalism in the Post–Uruguay Round Era: What Role for the EU? Netherlands Economic Institute, Rotterdam, May 12–13.

Tinbergen, J. 1956. *Economic Policy: Principles and Design.* Amsterdam: North Holland.

_____. 1952. *On the Theory of Economic Policy.* Amsterdam: North Holland.

Trela, I., and John Whalley. 1990. "Global Effects of Developed Country Trade Restrictions on Textiles and Apparel." *Economic Journal* 100(December), pp. 1190–1205.

UNCTAD. 1995. *Trade, Environment and Development: Lessons from Empirical Studies.* Synthesis report. New York and Geneva: United Nations.

_____. 1994. *Report on the Workshop Eco-Labeling and International Trade.* New York and Geneva: United Nations.

_____. 1993. *Liberalizing International Transactions in Services: A Handbook.* New York and Geneva: United Nations.

U.S. Department of Commerce. 1995. *The Big Emerging Markets.* Washington, D.C.: U.S. Department of Commerce.

Whalley, John. 1995. "Impact of the Multifibre Arrangement Phase Out on the Asian Economies." Unpublished manuscript.

_____. 1993. "Regional Trade Arrangements in North America: CUSTA and NAFTA." In Jaime De Melo and Arvind Panagariya, eds., *New Dimensions in Regional Integration.* Cambridge: Cambridge University Press, pp. 352–382.

Wilcox, Clair. 1949. *Charter for World Trade.* New York: Macmillan.

Winham, Gilbert. 1990. "GATT and the International Trade Regime." *International Journal* 45 (Autumn), pp. 796–822.

_____. 1989. "The Prenegotiation Phase of the Uruguay Round." In Janice Gross Stein, ed., *Getting to the Table.* Baltimore and London: Johns Hopkins University Press, pp. 44–67.

World Bank. 1995. *World Development Report.* New York: Oxford University Press.

_____. 1994. *World Development Report.* New York: Oxford University Press.

WTO. 1997. *Focus Newsletter* no. 15 (January).

_____. 1996a. *Focus Newsletter* no. 10 (May).

_____. 1996b. "The Road Ahead: International Trade Policy in the Era of the WTO." Fourth Annual Sylvia Ostry Lecture, Ottawa, May 28. WTO Press/49, May 29.

_____. 1996c. "Director-General's Speech to EU Trade Ministers in Dublin." WTO Press/56, September 18.

_____. 1996d. *Focus Newsletter* no. 11 (June-July).

_____. 1996e. "Trade and Foreign Direct Investment." WTO Press/57, October 9.

_____. 1995a. *Focus Newsletter* no. 2 (March-April).

_____. 1995b. *Focus Newsletter* no. 3 (May-June).

_____. 1995c. "Overview of Developments in International Trade and the Trading System." Annual report by the director-general, December.

_____. 1995d. *Regionalism and the World Trading System.* Geneva: World Trade Organization.

Yeats, A. 1997. "Does Mercosur's Trade Performance Raise Concerns About the Effects of Regional Trade Arrangements?" Policy research paper 1729, World Bank, Washington, D.C.

Index